RADICAL MONOTHEISM
AND
WESTERN CULTURE

LIBRARY OF THEOLOGICAL ETHICS

RADICAL MONOTHEISM
AND
WESTERN CULTURE

WITH SUPPLEMENTARY ESSAYS

H. Richard Niebuhr

Foreword by James M. Gustafson

Westminster/John Knox Press
Louisville, Kentucky

First Harper Torchbook edition published 1970 by Harper & Row, Publishers, Inc., New York, New York 10022. Westminster/John Knox Press edition published by arrangement with Harper San Francisco.

This book is printed on acid-free paper that meets the American National Standards Institute Z39.48 standard. ∞

Published by Westminster/John Knox Press
Louisville, Kentucky

PRINTED IN THE UNITED STATES OF AMERICA

9 8 7 6 5 4 3 2 1

Library of Congress Cataloging-in-Publication Data

Niebuhr, H. Richard (Helmut Richard), 1894–1962.
    Radical monotheism and western culture : with supplementary essays
    / H. Richard Niebuhr ; foreword by James M. Gustafson.
            p.   cm. — (Library of theological ethics)
    Originally published: New York : Harper, 1960.
    Includes bibliographical references and index.
    ISBN 0-664-25326-1 (alk. paper)

    1. Theology, Doctrinal.   2. Christian ethics—United Church of Christ
authors.   3. Monotheism.   4. Civilization, Occidental.   5. Christianity
and culture.   6. Religion and science.   I. Title.   II. Series.
BT78.N495   1993
230—dc20   93-22590

*Presented with thanks for
what they have taught me
to the young men and women
who have studied with me*

Contents

Library of Theological Ethics

GENERAL EDITORS' INTRODUCTION

The field of theological ethics possesses in its literature an abundant inheritance concerning religious convictions and the moral life, critical issues, methods, and moral problems. The Library of Theological Ethics is designed to present a selection of important texts that would otherwise be unavailable for scholarly purposes and classroom use. The series will engage the question of what it means to think theologically and ethically. It is offered in the conviction that sustained dialogue with our predecessors serves the interests of responsible contemporary reflection. Our more immediate aim in offering it, however, is to enable scholars and teachers to make more extensive use of classic texts as they train new generations of theologians, ethicists, and ministers.

The volumes included in the Library will comprise a variety of types. Some will make available English-language texts and translations that have fallen out of print; others will present new translations of texts previously unavailable in English. Still others will offer anthologies or collections of significant statements about problems and themes of special importance. We hope that each volume will encourage contemporary theological ethicists to remain in conversation with the rich and diverse heritage of their discipline.

ROBIN W. LOVIN
DOUGLAS F. OTTATI
WILLIAM SCHWEIKER

1

Foreword

H. Richard Niebuhr was working on several projects during the 1950s and until his sudden death in 1962. Theological education in North America is the beneficiary of his willingness to interrupt these projects and study it; out of that project came *The Purpose of the Church and Its Ministry: The Advancement of Theological Education,* co-authored with Daniel Day Williams and myself, and *The Ministry in Historical Perspectives,* co-edited with Williams. Another book, *Faith on Earth,* edited by Richard R. Niebuhr (New Haven, Conn.: Yale University Press, 1989), was in manuscript form and was set aside during 1954-55 when the study of theological education absorbed his full attention. The Montgomery Lectures, which form the main body of *Radical Monotheism and Western Culture,* were delivered in 1957 at the University of Nebraska in Lincoln. In May 1959 Niebuhr delivered the Robertson Lectures at the University of Glasgow, which were published posthumously as *The Responsible Self.* The proofs of *Radical Monotheism* were delivered to our home in Lund, Sweden, when the Niebuhrs visited us there between their time in Scotland and England and their trip to Bonn, Germany, where he received an honorary degree. *The Responsible Self* is only part of what he would have included in a more comprehensive book on Christian ethics, a book that hundreds of Yale Divinity School graduates awaited as the final form of his powerful lectures on that subject over many years. Manuscripts of Cole Lectures, delivered at Vanderbilt University, had not been revised at the time of his death. Also on the docket was his commitment to edit Jonathan Edwards's ethical writings, a task ably done by his former student Paul Ramsey, and published in 1989 after Ramsey's death.

The Montgomery Lectures were published in a softcover book by the University of Nebraska before the Harper edition came out with the "Supplementary Essays." The name of that lectureship is important: "On Contemporary Civilization." The place is important: a state university that had no religious studies department, and one that was particularly sensitive to real or presumed issues of the relations between church and state and of religion in public education. The ordering of the lectures, the topics of each one, the pattern of analysis in each, and the carefully chosen rhetoric all, I believe, were constructed with this particular audience in mind. We have the work of a theologian showing how theology can address matters it shares with other disciplines, and how it can shed light on other disciplines and public issues while maintaining its own integrity.

The Supplementary Essays were chosen by Niebuhr to accompany the Montgomery Lectures; from among many previously published and unpublished papers he had written these were the ones that he thought cohered with radical monotheism. As his own Acknowledgments indicate, "The Nature and Existence of God" was first published in 1943 and anticipated themes developed in later work. "Theology—Not Queen but Servant" was a lecture delivered at a convocation of the University of Chicago in August 1954 at which he and other distinguished theologians received honorary degrees in conjunction with the Assembly of the World Council of Churches held in Evanston during that same month. "The Center of Value," as he notes in his Acknowledgments, was first published in Ruth Nanda Anshen's edited volume of brief essays, *Moral Principles of Action*. I invite readers to look at the list of distinguished contributors Ms. Anshen enlisted. I name only some of them: Robert MacIver, Karl Jaspers, Jacques Maritain, Werner Jaeger, F.S.C. Northrop, Erich Fromm, Paul Weiss, Martin Buber, Jean Piaget, Martin D'Arcy, C. H. Dodd, Daisetz Suzuki, Swami Nikhilananda, Albert Schweitzer, Ralph Linton, and Paul Tillich. Anshen's book remains a treasure trove of capsules of how major intellectuals of the time thought about ethics. Niebuhr's interest in value theory went back decades; "The Center of Value" is a concise statement of his relational value theory, and fittingly it continues to be referred to both as a major source of understanding Niebuhr's work and as a resource for constructive interpretive purposes.

Many of the themes and issues addressed in *Radical Monotheism* can be found in various forms in other writings of Niebuhr's from this period. I cite only a few examples. The monotheistic critique of Bibliocentrism, ecclesiocentrism and Christocentrism one finds in this book occurs also in *The Purpose of the Church and Its Ministry* and was often overlooked by its many admiring readers and reviewers.

(I recall Niebuhr saying to me on his return from the Evanston Assembly of the World Council of Churches, with real passion, "Christ, Christ, Christ! Church, church, church! Nobody speaks about God anymore! When I was young it was religion, religion, religion!") The central theme of faith as confidence and as loyalty or fidelity, worked out in such richness in *Faith on Earth,* is expressed in many places. One can note a prescience in Niebuhr's thought if one remembers when he was first expressing the implications of these ideas for academic disciplines, including the sciences; historians and philosophers of science have more recently developed similar ideas at greater length and with more specificity with reference to particular fields of learning.

Throughout the Montgomery Lectures and the Supplementary Essays is what I interpret as a basic pattern of Niebuhr's presentations, whether addressed to a broad public or to its ecclesial participants. I find it in *The Meaning of Revelation,* in this book, in *The Responsible Self,* and in other places. Whether or not it was his intention as an author, one of the effects is to make theology and theological thinking *intelligible* by showing their continuities with other forms of thinking and activity; at the same time he reinterprets other forms of activity in the light of theology so that they are seen differently. The idea of revelation is not as esoteric as many stereotypes of it presume, nor as supernatural as many Christians believe it to be. Once that is established, the idea of a revelation for Christians can be made intelligible both to the skeptics and to those within the churches.

Faith is not esoteric, as the twofold structure of his exposition of it—confidence and loyalty, or fidelity—makes clear. Faith, in these senses, is present in probably all forms of activity—social life, politics, science, religion, and so on and on. Having made this point clear, Niebuhr can *describe* (and it is often more description than linear argument) what faith in God is. It is not in a fundamental way different from other loci of human faith, but it is different in its object of confidence and loyalty. Once this point is made, from a radical monotheistic faith the faiths of other activities are reinterpreted in a profoundly prophetic way. The limits of these other forms of faith, e.g., monotheism or polytheism, are demonstrated, and the limiting effects of their outcomes are developed.

The subtitle of *The Responsible Self* is "An Essay in Christian Moral Philosophy." He describes three different types of morality:

humans as makers, as citizens, and as answerers. This makes intelligible not only positions in moral philosophy but also ways in which moral life is conducted. Readers, whether they are Christian, Jewish, or nonreligious, can identify persons, and participation in events, in the light of these types in a way that discloses a variety of human experience and thinking. Once this point is made, Niebuhr can develop his argument for the preference of the ethics of responsibility (which includes accountability and responsiveness) as the more adequate one philosophically and theologically, and can show how Christian faith and language give responsibility a particular context, texture, and direction.

The persuasiveness of this procedure, if my interpretation is even partially correct, comes not from appeals to heteronomous authorities; the outcome is not justified by the procedures and standards that are often used in theology and theological ethics. Rather, the persuasiveness comes from the intelligibility, and from the applications of what is made intelligible to Christian life and thought and to other modes and loci of life and thought. Language is well chosen to avoid possible pitfalls to the reader; sometimes it is abstract, e.g., the choice of Principle of Being rather than Being. Sometimes it is more specific, e.g., showing the limits of Jesus-centrism and ecclesiocentrism. And the move to radical monotheism is not justified simply by tradition; it is shown to be a more than plausible, and perhaps for him necessary, conclusion from his interpretations of a variety of activities: moral, intellectual, and religious. Once this point is made, it becomes the piercing beam to criticize the outcomes of confidence and loyalty in less than God. Activities are "centric"; partial centers are limiting and distorting, and even dangerous—sociocentrism, biocentrism, or what have you. Radical theocentrism exposes the deficiencies of these other centers.

Evident throughout his career, and particularly in the writings of this period, is Niebuhr's concern for the relations of power and goodness in the principle of Being. One poignant discussion is from *Faith on Earth* (p. 100). "The question is always before us, Is Power good? Is it good to and for what it has brought into being?" The second question is "Whether goodness is powerful, whether it is not forever defeated in actual existence by loveless, thoughtless power." To bring the assurance that Power, God, is good, and goodness is powerful, Niebuhr throughout his writing appeals to the Christian story. This appeal is not as strongly stated in *Radical Monotheism* as it is in some passages in *Faith on Earth,* in *The Meaning of Revelation,* or in Appendix B of *The Responsible Self.* In the latter, for example, we read, "The ultimate power does manifest itself as the Father of Jesus Christ through his resurrection from death." "So we apprehend the way God is manifested not in creation and destruction but in these and resurrection, in the raising of the temporal to the eternal plane" (p. 177). Readers of Niebuhr have to remember the opening paragraph of this Foreword. *Radical Monotheism,* with its lesser emphasis on the Christian story as a source for the assurance that the ultimate power is good and that goodness is powerful, is not Niebuhr's only testimony. But note should also be made, even in the above quotations, that God is manifested in creation and destruction as well as in resurrection. Niebuhr's ethics are not an ethics of all things being made new in Christ. And anything stated Christologically has to point to the Father, to God.

When Niebuhr wrote, the concern for "theology and public discourse," which is prevalent as this Foreword is written, was not addressed per se. Neither H. Richard nor Reinhold Niebuhr provides us with a set of hermeneutical questions that theology has to answer before it can converse with secular disciplines or with practitioners of various other activities. And even in the Montgomery Lectures he was aware that there was not "the public" but rather particular publics of science, politics, etc. Niebuhr does not provide us with a theory about how it is possible to be a theologian, and more particularly a Christian theologian, and yet be in on "the conversation" with nonreligious persons or persons from other religions. We are not given meta-discourse by Niebuhr. We are not invited to a conversation about how theologians can converse with other people. In the Montgomery Lectures and the Supplementary Essays he simply engaged in "public discourse"—a term I place in quotation marks since it is foreign to my normal vocabulary.

Niebuhr, in effect, says that if one wants to write about theology and ethics in relation to science one reads as much as one can, is explicit about one's limitations, and then engages in an interpretation of scientific activity in the light of theology and theological ethics; the same for religion, or for politics, or for academic life in a twentieth-century university. If one chooses to address various academic disciplines and activities, or various aspects of civil society, one finds the points of commonality from which to make theology and theological ethics intelligible, and having done that, one shows how theology can in turn address these matters not only in negative criticism but also appreciatively.

Radical Monotheism, then, in my judgment, is of continuing significance not only for the substance of its various chapters but also for what I have interpreted as the basic pattern. If the Montgomery Lectures are not "public theology," nothing I have read is. If they are deficient because he does not explicate a method for doing "public theology," let the charge be made. But by their fruits we know them, and Niebuhr has given us a rich harvest worthy of continuing study—much richer than I find in hundreds of pages of meta-discourse that try to figure out how what he did can be done.

JAMES M. GUSTAFSON

Acknowledgments

THE following pages present in revised and expanded form the Montgomery Lectures on Contemporary Civilization which I gave at the University of Nebraska in 1957. I have divided the three lectures of the original course into six chapters. To them I have added as supplementary essays a few articles that expand or otherwise complement the ideas developed under the head of Radical Monotheism and Western Culture.

It is a pleasure on this occasion to recall the friendliness with which the University of Nebraska received me and to express again my thanks to the Chancellor, his colleagues of the faculty and, particularly, to my genial host, Professor Lane W. Lancaster, the chairman of the lectureship committee. I am indebted to them for the opportunity to develop these reflections and for the encouragement to commit them to print.

Grateful acknowledgment is also made to the editors of *The Journal of Religion* for permission to republish here the first of the supplementary essays, formerly entitled "Theology—Not Queen but Servant," from the January issue of 1955; to the editors of *Motive* for permission to republish the third of the supplementary essays, formerly entitled "The Nature and Existence of God," from the December issue of 1943; and to Ruth Nanda Anshen for permission to use again in this connection the article on "The Center of Value" which was published under her editorship in the volume, *Moral Principles of Action* (Harper & Brothers, 1952). The lecture on "Science in Conflict with Morality?" was originally given at St. John's College, Annapolis, Maryland, as part of a symposium on "The Scientist as Philosopher." President Richard D. Weigle of St. John's has allowed me to have the lecture printed in this book; for this also I am indebted.

The essays previously published have been somewhat revised but

9

not extensively. Perhaps I should have taken fuller cognizance of the explications and criticisms of my thought offered by former students of mine who honored me with the presentation of a *Festschrift* in the fall of 1957. But I hesitated to involve myself in the intramural discussion into which a reply to their observations and criticisms tended to lead me and have therefore confined myself to efforts to state my thought a little more clearly. In dedicating this volume to the authors of *Faith and Ethics* and to their fellow students in my classes I apologize to them for being as recalcitrant in hewing to my own line as I often found them to be in following their own bent. For the encouragement they have given me to persevere in the development of my thought on Christian ethics I am immensely grateful. Perhaps a later work of mine, should it be forthcoming, may show greater results of their labors on my behalf than this one does.

H. RICHARD NIEBUHR

New Haven, Connecticut

I

Introduction: Theology and Faith

A THEOLOGIAN, asked to address himself to the subject of contemporary civilization for the purpose of generating constructive thought on its problems, may be expected to speak about the role of religion in modern society.[1] But when I reflect on the present human situation it is the problem of faith that presents itself to me as of the greatest importance; and faith is to be distinguished from religion. We express it in our religion, to be sure; but also in all our other social decisions, actions, and institutions. Furthermore, our whole culture is involved in a conflict of faiths that is distinctly different from the collisions among religions or between religion and irreligion. In the following reflections I shall try to analyze this conflict as one between radical monotheism and the other main forms of human faith, namely, polytheism and henotheism in their modern, nonmythological guise. The chief rival to monotheism, I shall contend, is henotheism or that social faith which makes a finite society, whether cultural or religious, the object of trust as well as of loyalty and which tends to subvert even officially monotheistic institutions, such as the churches.

1. THE DUAL TASK OF THEOLOGY

Before I begin this analysis, however, it seems appropriate that I should define my conception of the theologian's task. Apparently his title defines it and fixes his responsibility. Is he not to be concerned with the *logos* or theory of God as the psychologist is concerned with the *logos* of the *psyche* and the archaeologist with the theoretic understanding of ancient monuments? As soon as we

---

[1] Acceptance of appointment to the Montgomery Lectureship includes acceptance of the provision that "the purpose of the lectures is to generate constructive thought on contemporary problems."

so formulate the question and the answer we are made aware of the difficulties that have involved theology in many historic conflicts. The word *theos* directs us indeed toward an object but not quite in the same way that *anthropos* does in anthropology or *geos* in geology. It is the name for that objective being, that other-than-the-self, which men have before them as they *believe* rather than as they *see*, hear, feel, or even as they reason. This objective reality—God or the gods—is acknowledged or known in faith we say. To be sure, there are philosophers who develop a theory of God without reference to faith but the relation of their metaphysics or ontologies to the theologies of faith remains the subject of many discussions.[2]

At all events theology, in distinction from though not necessarily in opposition to metaphysics and ontology, has been unable to abstract discourse about the objective reality, God, from discourse about the subjective activity of faith, however the latter is defined. Hence a strong temptation arose in some periods, particularly in nineteenth-century Protestant theology, to drop the objective side of theological inquiry in favor of a psychology of faith or a psychology of religion which considers only the subjective element. But now it has become quite clear—in human existence no less than in academic inquiry—that the subjective can no more be meaningfully abstracted from the objective than vice versa. Theology must attend to the God of faith if it is to understand faith no less than it must attend to faith in God if it would understand God. Faith is at least as much an unavoidable counterpart of the presence of God as sense experience is an unavoidable counterpart of the presence of natural entities or powers. The analogy is inadequate; pressed too far it is misleading. Faith is not a special sense; faith and sense experience are not exclusive of each other; the objective

2 "The God of Aristotle," writes Professor Arthur O. Lovejoy, "had almost nothing in common with the God of the Sermon on the Mount—though, by one of the strangest and most momentous paradoxes in Western history, the philosophical theology of Christendom identified them, and defined the chief end of man as the imitation of both" (*The Great Chain of Being*, 1936, p. 5). Many a theologian agrees. "I certainly see," writes Karl Barth, "that such a science (i.e., natural theology or a knowledge of God and his connection with the world and men apart from revelation) does exist, but I do not see how it is possible for it to exist. I am convinced that so far as it has existed at all and still exists, it owes its existence to a radical error" (*The Knowledge of God and the Service of God*, 1938, pp. 4 and 5). In the debates about the relations of philosophical theology to the theology of faith or of revelation such extreme positions are, of course, often challenged from both sides; but they indicate the nature of the issues.

reality present to faith is not irrelevant to the objects of sense experience. But faith and God belong together somewhat as sense experience and physical reality do. Hence when we carry on theological work we must do so as men who participate in faith, who exercise faith even while they are criticizing it, who are reflective about faith in their reflections on God, the object of faith.

If that first point be at least tentatively accepted until we can endeavor to illuminate the character of faith, we may move on to the second. Reason and faith are not exclusive of each other; reasoning is present in believing and one task of theology is to develop such reasoning in faith. The inadequate analogy of sense experience and faith may again be used to illustrate the point. We do not generally regard sense experience and reason as exclusive of each other, however great our participation may be in philosophical debates between radical empiricism and rationalism, or however important we find the disputes about the relative values of inductive and deductive reasoning or about the functions of hypotheses in empirical science. Bare sense experience unmixed with rational elements is inaccessible to us; reason forms and interprets sense experience; experience validates or invalidates such experience-filled reasoning. In roughly analogous manner reason permeates the activity of faith; it organizes, compares, reflects, criticizes, and develops hypotheses in the midst of believing.

An example of such reasoning in faith may be found in the 8th Psalm, though almost any other expression of faith could be used as illustration.

O Lord, our Lord, how majestic is thy name in all the earth! Thou whose glory above the heavens is chanted by the mouths of babes and infants, thou hast founded a bulwark because of thy foes, to still the enemy and the avenger. When I look at thy heavens, the work of thy fingers, the moon and the stars which thou hast established; what is man that thou art mindful of him, and the son of man that thou dost care for him? Yet thou hast made him little less than God, and dost crown him with glory and honor. Thou hast given him dominion over the works of thy hand; thou hast put all things under his feet. . . .

Most readers of this prayer of adoration will probably agree in accepting it as an expression of faith, however they may vary in their definitions of faith or in their analyses of the relations between the poetic form and the faith attitude of the prayer. They will note that the worshiper's mind does not move from reason to faith; it does not proceed along a path of inferential reasoning from empirically known earth and heavens to an unknown Creator and thence toward confidence in him as the source of good. The movement begins in faith, with God, and so proceeds toward the visible world. But reason is present in this faith. First of all it appears as a kind of aesthetic reason which intuits the intention of the divine artist in the wholeness of his masterpieces; but it is present also as analytic, comparing, and relating reason, as distinguishing and question-raising, even as doubting reason. Reasoning faith, confident in God as the source of the glory as well as of the being of all creatures, makes its distinctions and comparisons among celestial and mundane, human and subhuman beings. It doubts the value of man, related not only to God but to these other works of his. It asks questions about man's significance in the cosmos. It finds answers with the aid of analogical thinking: man in relation to the animals is something like God in his relation to the world. In this movement of the mind the confidence in God is never questioned: faith is not being supported by reason; rather, faith reasons and faith doubts in its reasoning. It doubts some beliefs about God and about man and seeks surer beliefs. So the faith expressing itself in devotion and wonder is a reasoning faith.

Now one task of theology is to develop this reasoning in faith. Hence it often undertakes to ask and answer, within the context of faith, the Psalmist's question, What is man in the world of which God is the principle? Or it seeks to answer within this context questions implicit in the faith utterance about the mode and meaning of God's creation of the cosmos, about the destructive elements in it or beyond it. Such theological theory presupposes faith, but must develop the rational elements in it. As expressions of faith the statements of such theology will almost always be somewhat inferior to the utterances of poets and prophets. A theologian qua theologian could no more have written the 8th Psalm than archaeologist qua archaeologist could have written "Ode on a Grecian Urn"; yet the theologian's development of the reasoning in faith is no less closely related to faith than is the Psalmist's development of the aesthetic form. His work is work of reason in the context of faith. God is the ultimate object of his inquiry, but, of course, God as present to faith.

The second task for which theology, or a part of it, is responsible is the criticism of faith, not as a subjective attitude or activity only but in relation to its objects. In this work theology is related to faith somewhat as literary criticism is related to poetic action and expression. Here again participation is indispensable. The literary critic must know by direct participation what the aesthetic experience is, what poetic creation requires in the way of both inspiration and labor, and what sort of movement takes place in the poet's mind between sensuous symbol and meaning. He must live in the same world of values in which the poet lives. Unless he is himself something of a poet how can the critic illuminate, analyze, and discipline poetry? The theological critic of faith is in a similar situation. Without participation in the life of faith he cannot distinguish between its high and low, genuine and spurious experiences and expressions, between symbol and meaning. But as the work of literary critics presupposes and is ancillary to the work of poets, so the activity of theologians is secondary to that of believers. As critical theologians they are concerned with the knowledge of God; hence their interest is directed more toward the faith to which God or the gods are present than toward God and the gods. Yet they could not be critical, they could not illuminate and seek to bring order into the life of faith, unless they participated in faith's apprehension of its object.

Thus theology, as disciplined development of the reasoning that permeates faith and as critique of faith, must always participate in the activity of faith, though its ultimate concern is with God. As an effort of disciplined thinking in this context it cannot easily be classified under one of the current great categories of human inquiry: as a science, or as one of the humanities, or as history, or as a *Geisteswissenschaft*, or as a critique or a philosophy. It must develop its own methods in view of the situation in which it works and of the object with which it deals, without becoming the vassal of methodologies developed by rational inquiries directed toward other objects and existing in connection with other nonrational activities of men besides faith. Neither queen nor vassal among such inquiries, it must pursue its own way in service of the God of faith and of his servants. That way, though independent, cannot be the way of isolation, unless the theology in question be concerned with some constricted, divisive faith, directed toward a little god, toward one among many objects of human devotion rather than with the faith that is directed toward the One beyond the many, in whom the many are one.

2. Faith As Confidence and Fidelity

Having described theology as inseparably connected with faith we need further to preface our effort to develop theological reflections on civilization by defining *faith*. The word is used for many purposes as the dictionaries make evident; with its aid we refer to many attitudes and actions of persons and communities. Sometimes it is the equivalent of another multimeaninged term, *religion*, as when we speak of the "faiths of mankind"; sometimes it is synonymous with assurance of any sort as in the phrase "animal faith"; often it signifies belief or creed, as when Alexander Pope writes,

> For modes of faith let graceless zealots fight;
> His can't be wrong whose life is in the right.

It may be that indiscriminate use of the word has deprived it of a fairly precise original meaning or that the variety of meanings is due to the fact that we are dealing with a kind of complex structure of which now this, now that part is called to attention, as is the case, for instance, when we use "morality" to mean conformity to the *mores*, the *mores* themselves, instruction in the *mores*, etc. But avoiding the semantic problem we may undertake to describe a fundamental personal attitude which, whether we call it *faith* or give it some other name, is apparently universal or general enough to be widely recognized. This is the attitude and action of confidence in, and fidelity to, certain realities as the sources of value and the objects of loyalty. This personal attitude or action is ambivalent; it involves reference to the value that attaches to the self and to the value toward which the self is directed. On the one hand it is trust in that which gives value to the self; on the other hand it is loyalty to what the self values. Friendship may be taken as a simple example of such an ambivalent relation. In friendship I believe in my friend as one who values me; I have confidence in him that he will continue to regard me as valuable; I also value him and am loyal to him. Insofar as faith is present in friendship it is a double movement of trust in the friend who is a source of my value and of loyalty to him as value objective to me.

A better example may be found in nationalism. When the patriotic nationalist says "I was born to die for my country" he is exhibiting the double relation that we now call faith. The national life is for him the reality whence his own life derives its worth. He relies on the nation as source of his own value. He trusts it; first, perhaps, in the sense of looking constantly to it as the enduring reality out of which he has issued, into whose ongoing cultural life his own actions and being will merge. His life has meaning because it is part of that context, like a word in a sentence. It has value because it fits into a valuable whole. His trust may also be directed toward the nation as a power which will supply his needs, care for his children, and protect his life. But faith in the nation is primarily reliance upon it as an enduring value-center. Insofar as the nation is the last value-center to which the nationalist refers, he does not raise the question about its goodness to him or about its rightness or wrongness. Insofar as it is value-center rightness and wrongness depend on it. This does not mean in any Hobbesian sense that for such faith the national government determines what is right and what is wrong but rather that the rightness of all actions depends on their consonance with the inner constitution of the nation and on their tendency to enhance or diminish national life, power, and glory.

On this source of value the consistent nationalist depends not only for his own meaning but for the worth of everything else he encounters. So far as he is consistent even his wife and children will have their ultimate worth not because of their relation to him but by virtue of their relation to the fatherland. Even his personal enemies will have some worth so long as they are citizens. Cultural goods—paintings, sculpture, poetry, music—will be valued as creations of the nation, embodiments of its spirit; economic activities and goods as expressions of the communal élan. Religion and education will be no less dependent for their significance on the extent to which they image the creative source. To be sure, all these goods will also be valued instrumentally by the nationalist; he will ask about their meaning as effective contributions to the continuing life of his country. Yet their goodness like his own is first of all not so much "good-forness" as "good-fromness." They are meaningful because what the nation means is expressed in them, not because they refer to the nation. So faith in the nation is reliance on it as value-center or value-source.[3]

The counterpart of trust in the value-center is loyalty or fidelity. Trust is, as it were, the passive aspect of the faith relation. It is expressed in praise or confessed in a creed that states the self-evident principle. Loyalty or faithfulness is the active side. It values the center and seeks to enhance its power and glory. It makes that center its cause for which to live and labor. In this active faith the loyal self organizes its activities and seeks to organize its world. Faith-loyalty, though it use the same words as faith-trust, expresses itself in a sacramentum, an oath of fealty, a vow of commitment. Thus the creedal expressions of patriotism, uttered or heard in one way, seem to state with simple assurance and as matters of fact that Britain rules the waves, or that Germany is over all, or that Columbia is the home of the brave and the free. Yet these same phrases are also used to pledge devotion; they are spoken and sung by voices ringing with resolution; they may signalize decision to give everything to the country's cause. So also the Christian statement, "I believe in God, the Father, Almighty Maker of heaven and earth," is on the one hand an expression of confidence, on the other, an oath of allegiance. In the one sense it means, "I trust in God"; in the other, "I will keep faith with him."

The two aspects of faith illustrated in the dual meaning of creeds and in the character of nationalism can be more fully explored with the aid of two thinkers: Tolstoi and Royce. In Tolstoi's analysis of faith attention is directed to the importance for life of confidence in a value-center. In Royce's philosophy of loyalty the meaning of faithfulness is explored. But that these two things belong together in life also becomes apparent.

In our effort to understand faith Tolstoi's story may have for us a value similar to the value of Descartes' story for an inquiry into the nature of knowledge. As Descartes began with doubt of all received opinion that passed for knowledge, so Tolstoi began with shaken confidence in all accepted faiths in life's meaning; as the former worked his way through skepticism to assured knowledge so

[3] For illustration of nationalist faith see Carleton J. H. Hayes, *Essays on Nationalism*, 1928, pp. 104 ff.; also Salo W. Baron, *Modern Nationalism and Religion*, 1947, especially Chap. II.

the latter refused to abandon his search for value until he found a solid basis for confidence.

In *My Confession* Tolstoi traced first of all the story of faith-gods that failed.

Christened and educated in Russian Orthodox Christianity he had by the age of eighteen discarded all that he had been taught. Later when he reflected on his youth it seemed to him that all he had at that time in the way of a belief that gave shape to life, apart from mere animal instinct, had been a kind of idealistic belief in the possibility of perfection. This had merged into the desire to be admired by his fellow men, first for his moral qualities but then for power, distinction, and wealth. His early success as a writer had brought him into the company of the artists, who believed in the development of mankind and regarded themselves as the principal agents in that progress. Though they thought of themselves as teachers of men they did not ask what they had to teach; they assumed that somehow, unconsciously, they made great contributions to progress. "The faith in poetry and the development of life," said Tolstoi, "was a true faith and I was one of its priests. To be one of its priests was very advantageous and agreeable." But this faith also crumbled. The quarrels and immoralities of the artists, the sight of an execution that brought home the superstitious character of the belief in progress, the death of a brother "who died without understanding why he had lived and still less what his death meant for him"—these shook the confidence that had taken the place of childhood faith. Then came marriage and for a time family priesthood took the place of literary priesthood. "The effort to effect my own individual perfection, already replaced by the striving after general progress, was again changed into an effort to secure the particular happiness of my family." Then this confidence that his existence and work were important because they contributed to family welfare also became dubious. So life came to a stop. At every point the question "But why?" or, as we might say, "So what?" intruded itself into Tolstoi's deliberations. Whether he thought about his estate, about the thousands of acres and the hundreds of horses he owned, or about the education of his children, or about his literary activities, he always returned to the question of meaning. So what? "What if I should be more famous than Gogol, Pushkin, Shakespeare, Molière—than all the writers of the world—well, and what then?" He felt, he wrote, that the ground on which he stood was crumbling, that what he had been living for was nothing, that he had no reason for living.[4]

"The truth was," said Tolstoi, "that life was meaningless." Sometimes it seemed to him that it "was a foolish and wicked joke" played on him by someone, though he did not believe in a Creator. Or he felt orphaned, isolated, like a fledgling thrown from the nest —but by whom?

After many years, and much seeking for wisdom in science, philosophy, and religion, he came again to confidence in life's meaning, to zest in worthwhile labors. But the new faith was very different from that of the child, that of the artist, or that of the family man; and its labors were directed toward other ends. The creed in which it was expressed was a highly personal one, but it was both an expression of confidence and an oath of allegiance.

Among the things Tolstoi had discovered in the course of his loss of faith and of his recovery was a general truth: "I was compelled to admit," he wrote, "that besides the reasoning knowledge which I once thought was the only true knowledge, there was in every living man another kind of knowledge, an unreasoning one,—faith, —which gives the possibility of living. . . . From the beginning of the human race, wherever there is life there is faith which makes life possible, and everywhere the leading characteristics of faith are the same. Whatever answers any kind of faith ever gives to any one, every one of these answers gives an infinite meaning to the finite life of man, a meaning which is not destroyed by suffering, privation and death. . . . Faith is the knowledge of the meaning of human life, in consequence of which man does not destroy himself but lives. Faith is the force of life. If a man lives he believes in something. If he did not believe there was something to live for, he would not live. If he does not see and understand the unreality of the finite, he believes in the finite; if he sees that unreality, he must believe in the infinite. Without faith it is impossible to live."[5]

However many aspects of the complex personal or communal attitude and action called *faith* Tolstoi's confession may leave out of account, it does bring into focus one specific element in that

---

[4] Doubtless this depression in Tolstoi's middle age has a clinical history; but the kind of normality that never asks these questions has no less of a clinical history. And thoughtful psychologists as well as philosophers have often pointed out that truth and health are not always mutually supporting values.

[5] Lyof N. Tolstoi, *My Confession*, Chap. IX.

complex: the dependence of a living self on centers of value whence it derives its worth and for the sake of which it lives. Moreover, the story of Tolstoi's life illustrates what is well known from experience and observation—that there is movement in existence from one center to another, that the centers are frequently ill-defined, and that often they are communities, such as mankind or the family.

In Tolstoi's understanding of faith confidence in a source of value is stressed, though his writings and his action make clear that the movement of fidelity to that source as chosen cause is also present. In Josiah Royce's philosophy of loyalty this other side of faith is given first importance. Royce's argument is a double one: first, that the essence of the moral life is loyalty to a cause; secondly, that the true cause is loyalty itself. The second argument does not now concern us but the first seems cogent whether or not it is followed by the second. Royce finds the kind of loyalty he speaks of illustrated in the faithfulness of ordinary folk who do their duty, sometimes in such a way that their heroism is celebrated, more often unspectacularly. It is present in warriors who live by the same devotion in peace as in war and who honor like-minded loyalty in their enemies; in martyrs who die for their faith; in patient mothers and fathers who toil in true devotion for their homes; in "the calm and laborious devotion to a science which has made possible the life-work of a Newton or of a Maxwell, or of a Darwin."[6] The causes to which loyal men commit themselves are various, but the spirit of fidelity, or its form, is always the same.

There is a marked parallelism between the movement of loyalty, as Royce describes it, and the story of confidence as illustrated by Tolstoi. Youth begins its moral development within the matrix of a society whose laws, customs, and authoritative social will challenge the individual to revolt and to self-assertion. Moral maturity comes when individual self-will gives way to a loyalty that, freely choosing a larger cause, unifies self and world in its service. "A loyal man is one who has found and who sees, neither mere individual fellow-men to be loved or hated, nor mere conventions nor customs, nor laws to be obeyed, but some social cause or system of causes, so rich, so well-knit, and, to him, so fascinating and withal so kindly in its appeal to his natural self-will, that he says to his cause: 'Thy

[6] *The Sources of Religious Insight*, 1912, pp. 190-97.

will is mine and mine is thine. In thee I do not lose but find myself, living intensely in proportion as I live for thee."[7] Account must be taken of the fact that "devoted people have often been loyal to very bad causes; or that different people have been loyal to causes which were in deadly war with one another"; but these defects of loyalty leave "still untouched the one great fact, that if you want to find a way of living which surmounts doubts, and centralizes your powers, it must be some such a way as all the loyal in common have trodden, since first loyalty was known among men."[8] We may state the case somewhat more strongly than Royce does, saying that selfhood and loyalty go together; that however confused the loyalties of selves may be, however manifold their causes and however frequent their betrayals, yet it is by fidelity that they live no less than by confidence in centers of value which bestow worth on their existence. Centers of value and causes may, however, be only two names for the same objective realities from which and for which selves live as valued and valuing beings.

It may be too bold to assert that such relations of faith are universal among human selves, yet it is significant that the dual faith relation makes its appearance even in the expressions of those men who are most skeptical of the meaningfulness of such terms as "faith" and "value." In the case of a few of these disvaluers of "value" and unbelievers in "faith" it seems that the community and activity of exact, empirical science is the source of value whence all other activity and existence derive meaning; it is also a cause which they espouse and serve. Whatever philosophical endeavors do not depend upon or contribute to "scientific truth" such men tend to regard as valueless if not as mischievous. Whatever artistic, religious, or educational activities are not interpretable by reference to that center, either as illustrative of the search for such truth or as contributory to it, are likely to be regarded as meaningless. Yet their own activity, it is clear, is esteemed to be valuable because it participates in and serves the movement and community of empirical science. Dispassionate about everything else they espouse their cause with passion. Others—and they are the larger number among those who are skeptical about "faith" and "value,"—do ask

[7] *The Philosophy of Loyalty*, 1908, p. 43. Royce developed the same theme in *The Sources of Religious Insight*, Chap. V, and in *The Problem of Christianity*, 1913, Vol. I, Lectures III and IV.
[8] *Philosophy of Loyalty*, pp. 45, 46.

the question about what science itself is good for, whence it derives its value, and what cause it serves. Their answer sometimes is that it serves the cause of biological life and they do not raise the further question about the value of life.[9]

In every attack on specific loyalties and systems of valuation and even in every attack on the double principle of faith itself some faith is manifested, some dependence on a value-center, some loyalty to a cause.

Most revealing of the nature of faith is the negative literature of disillusionment. When the failure of the gods is described, when treason is examined, or when atheistic existentialism tries to find a center of value in the bare self in its self-making freedom we become conscious of the apparently universal human necessity of faith and of the inescapability of its gods, not as supernatural beings but as value-centers and objects of devotion.

[9] E.g., the first edition of A. J. Ayer's *Language, Truth and Logic*, 1936. See Chap. VI and pp. 48, 58, 139.

II

The Idea of Radical Monotheism

---

1. THE SOCIAL GOD AND THE MANY GODS

In ordinary discourse the word "gods" has many meanings. Now we mean by it the powers on which men call for help in time of trouble; now the forces which they summon up in their search for ecstasy; now the realities before which they experience awe and the sense of the holy; now the beings they posit in their speculative efforts to explain the origin and government of things; now the objects of adoration. The question whether religion in which all these attitudes and activities are present is a single movement of the mind and with it the query whether the word "gods" refers to entities of one class, must be left to other contexts. We are concerned now with faith as dependence on a value-center and as loyalty to a cause. Hence when we speak of "gods" we mean the gods of faith, namely, such value-centers and causes.

In this narrowed sense the plural term "gods" seems alone appropriate. The religious and also the political institutions of the West have long been officially monotheistic, so that we do not easily regard ourselves as polytheists, believers in many gods, or as henotheists, loyal to one god among many. Using the word "god" without definition we regard ourselves as either theists or atheists. But if we confine our inquiry to the forms of faith, then it seems more true to say that monotheism as value dependence and as loyalty to One beyond all the many is in constant conflict among us with the two dominant forms: a pluralism that has many objects of devotion and a social faith that has one object, which is, however, only one among many. If by gods we mean the objects of such faith then atheism seems as irreconcilable with human existence as is radical skepticism in the actuality of the things we eat, and breathe, walk upon and bump into. Atheism in this sense is no more a live

24

alternative for us in actual personal existence, than psychological solipsism is in our physical life. To deny the reality of a supernatural being called God is one thing; to live without confidence in some center of value and without loyalty to a cause is another.

The historically and biographically primitive form of faith seems to be the henotheistic, or social, type though it has often been argued that the historic movement is from pluralism to the relative unity of a socially organized loyalty. Whatever temporal progressions there may be, most frequently in past and present the two forms exist in uneasy rivalry with, and accommodation to, each other. We may begin with henotheism of which the nationalism we previously used to illustrate faith is a characteristic representative. Instead of the nation some smaller social unit—family or tribe or sectarian community—or a larger one—civilization or humanity—may constitute the center of value and the cause of loyalty. In any case, where such faith prevails the ultimate reference in all answers to questions about the meaning of individual life and about the cause for which one lives, is made, in Bergson's phrase, to some closed society.[1] Such a society may number among its members the dead and the yet unborn as well as the living, supernatural as well as natural existences, animals (totem animals, for instance) as well as men, natural phenomena—wind and sky and thunder—as well as animate beings. But every participant in the group derives his value from his position in the enduring life of the community. Here he is related to an actuality that transcends his own, that continues to be though he ceases to exist. He is dependent on it as it is not dependent on him. And this applies even more to his significance than to his existence. The community is not so much his great good as the source and center of all that is good, including his own value. But the society is also his cause; its continuation, power, and glory are the unifying end of all his actions. The standard by which he judges himself and his deeds, his companions and their actions, by which also he knows himself to be judged, is the standard of loyalty to the community.

Such faith, like any faith, is exhibited not only in religious beliefs and practices but it does manifest itself in these. The sociological analysis of religion is therefore so persuasive because the kind of

---

[1] In his *The Two Sources of Morality and Religion*, 1932, Henri Bergson described the religion of humanity as that of an open, not closed, society. This interpretation seems highly questionable, see p. 35.

faith most frequently associated with religion is of the social sort. "The idea of society," says Durkheim, "is the soul of religion." The gods of religion, he maintains—though not without difficulties in view of the protean character of gods—are collective representations. By this he means, first, that they are ideas imposed on individual minds by the group; secondly, and more significantly, that "they not only come from the collective but the things which they express are of a social nature." The reality which "mythologies have represented under so many different forms but which is the universal and eternal objective cause of these sensations *sui generis* out of which religious experience is made, is society." Striking examples of the socially representative character of mythical gods or divine powers are to be found in Vesta, the domestic fire, in Themis, the projection into the cosmos of the social law, in the identification of Osiris with the Egyptian ruler, in the deification of ancestral heroes and Roman emperors. But there are even more significant though less immediately clear illustrations of the expression of social faith in religious mythologies and cults.[2] Hence it is possible to describe many movements in the history of religion by reference to the growth of society from simple and constricted to complex and more inclusive groupings. Though not all religions nor all aspects of any particular religion are explicable by means of Durkheim's formula, it does have wide applicability because of the prevalence of social faith.

Not only religion, however, indicates the actuality of the henotheism that makes society, usually in the guise of a symbol, the value-center and object of loyalty. This form of faith is expressed with equal frequency in moral behavior: in obedience to written and unwritten social laws, in the sense of merit and of guilt before social authority; in the definitions of good and of right encountered in many a critical analysis of morality. When men's ultimate orientation is in their society, when it is their value-center and cause, then the social mores can make anything right and anything wrong; then indeed conscience is the internalized voice of society or of its representatives. The sociological interpreters of ethics are as persuasive as the sociological interpreters of religion, because for so many human beings, or for all of us at so many times, the implicit or explicit faith that underlies our ethos and ethics is the social faith

[2] E. Durkheim, *The Elementary Forms of Religious Life*, n.d., pp. 417-19; cf. also F. M. Cornford, *From Religion to Philosophy*, 1912.

whose god (value-center and cause) is society itself. From this one source we derive whatever unity there is in our evaluations and our behavior.

Where this faith is dominant art also may have its focus in the society. Hence patriotic art is always popular with its symbolism of the national spirit, with themes taken from the social myth or history, with its enhancement of the glory of national existence.

Henotheistic faith, usually described only as a phenomenon of primitive social life or of childhood, living in the matrix of family, evidently pervades the modern world in the form of nationalism. Its fanatical extremes, encountered in German National Socialism and Italian Fascism, have called to our attention more moderate manifestations in which some polytheism or some movements toward monotheism qualify the central devotion. Nationalism shows its character as a faith whenever national welfare or survival is regarded as the supreme end of life; whenever right and wrong are made dependent on the sovereign will of the nation, however determined; whenever religion and science, education and art, are valued by the measure of their contribution to national existence. By these tests nationalist faith shows its pervasive presence to us in our common life every day in schools and churches no less than in political utterances and policies.

The prevalence of social henotheism may be illustrated, however, also by reference to its nonnationalist versions. Whether or not Marxism is a religion may be disputed, but that it is a faith in the sense in which we are using the term seems very clear. Its ethics is class ethics, its art class art.[3] Its conflict with nationalism in our time is the conflict of one social faith with another, though by and large even in the sphere of Communist rule the greater potency of nationalism as a faith has been demonstrated. Another nonnationalist henotheism makes civilization its Alpha and Omega. Though a civilization is a larger community than nation it also remains a closed society; it is always one among many. Where it

[3] "Very frequently," said Lenin, "the bourgeoisie makes the charge that we Communists deny all morality. . . . In what sense do we deny ethics, morals? . . . We deny all morality taken from super-human or non-class conceptions. We say that this is a deception, a swindle, a befogging of the minds of the workers and peasants in the interests of the landlords and capitalists. We say that our morality is wholly subordinate to the interests of the class-struggle of the proletariat. We deduce our morality from the facts and needs of the class-struggle of the proletariat." V. I. Lenin, *Religion* (Little Lenin Library, Vol. 7), 1933, pp. 47 f.

is the value-center and the cause then science and religion, art and economics, political and economic institutions, ethos and ethics, are valued as manifestations of the ongoing life of the civilized society or as contributions toward its survival and enhancement. Religious communities, also, that are professedly monotheistic may, as we shall see, revert to a henotheism in which God is the name given to the principle of the religious group itself as a closed society.

The great alternative to henotheism with its relative unification of life is pluralism in faith and polytheism among the gods. Historically and in the contemporary scene such pluralism seems most frequently to follow on the dissolution of social faith. When confidence in nation or other closed society is broken, men who must live by faith take recourse to multiple centers of value and scatter their loyalties among many causes. When the half-gods go the minimal gods arrive. Faith in the social value-center may be dissolved in acids produced in many bitter experiences. Internal conflicts, the recognition that the social loyalties are being used to further the interests of power-seeking individuals or groups; the revelation that the apparently unified society is without integrity; the rational dissolution of social mythologies; encounters with other societies superior in power or glory; eventually, the breakup of a community or its disappearance into some larger mass—these shatter the confidence that life is worthwhile as lived from and toward the communal center. The natural, perennial faith of men in the society in which they were born—whose authority governed them, whose laws protected them, whose language gave them their logic, which nurtured them in life and by remembrance maintains them in death, for whose sake they reared their children, labored and fought—evermore comes to a cheerless end among large and little, conscious and unconscious treasons, or among natural and political disasters, encountered or foreseen. It is in such a situation that man's other faith, polytheism, never wholly suppressed even in the midst of his social loyalties, is likely to become dominant.

To be sure, among the most critical and most self-conscious men the dissolution of communal faith may call forth an effort to substitute self for society, to make isolated selfhood both value-center and cause. Epicureanism and existentialism exemplify such an effort. In the former the self seems to seek its center within itself but really finds it in something imposed on the self, the pain-and-pleasure feeling that is the constant accompaniment of conscious existence. On this dual sentiency all that is valuable and disvaluable depends. Pleasurable existence even becomes a kind of cause, since the reasoning self is now required to organize its activities toward the maintenance and enhancement of a pleasurable state of feeling; it is even guilty before itself when it allows itself to be swayed by passion to seek illusory pleasures that are followed by pain. Moreover, this sad philosophy of life is overshadowed at all times by the inescapable realities of pain and of death. If pleasure makes life worth living, pain makes it not only valueless but disvaluable, while the death of the self is the end of all transient value and disvalue. Existentialism is a more robust assertion of faith seeking a center in the self and a cause projected by a self. In its most radical form it has man making himself "man in order to be God" and "losing himself in order that the self-cause may exist."[4] Such extreme existentialism seems to represent the dying effort of the self to maintain itself by faith—but now by faith in nothing. Its confidence is not the confidence *in* the self but *of* a self, and it is confidence in nothing; its cause is not *the* self but the self projecting itself toward nothing.

Epicureanism and existentialism look like ghostly survivals of faith among men who, forsaken by the gods, continue to hold on to life. The more common alternative to communal confidence and loyalty appears in that less radical egoism in which an unintegrated, diffuse self-system depends for its meanings on many centers and gives its partial loyalties to many interests. This is polytheism whatever mythology accompany the pluralistic faith. In it a break has occurred between the centers of values and the causes which for henotheism were one. Now men look for their worth to various beings, human and superhuman, who value them or from whom by effort they can extract some recognition of value. The old sense that the self is important because it is and exists as part of one enduring community is replaced by the feeling that it is justified in living only insofar as it can prove its worth. In times when supernatural beings are thought to regard the actions of men, value dependence becomes a frantic effort to satisfy these gods that the believer is worthy of their attention. When there are no supernatural beings in one's world then the proof of worth must be offered to other humans, to the prestige persons in one's environ-

[4] Jean-Paul Sartre, *Being and Nothingness*, 1956, p. 626.

ment. These become the centers of valuation. Their presence is supplemented by beings to whom the self looks for unmerited recognition. The need to be valued for one's own sake rather than for one's achievements may manifest itself in restless searching for transient lovers; it may also appear in the cultivation of a piety that looks to the Deity or deities of established religion for love while it scarcely thinks of them as causes requiring loyalty. Within Christendom Jesus as the lover of the soul, a kind heavenly Father, a comforting Holy Spirit, a compassionate Virgin, may play roles in such piety that are hard to distinguish religiously, morally, or psychologically, from the roles of guardian spirits in other societies. They are looked to for assurance of worth, while the self continues to pursue interests of many sorts and gives its fragmented loyalty to many causes.

For as the sources of value are many in polytheism so are the causes. These, however, are no longer realities requiring unified fidelity; they have become interests that from moment to moment attract vagrant potencies resident in the mind and body. To be sure, their objective nature may be posited; they may be given semipersonal names, such as Truth, Beauty, Justice, Peace, Love, Goodness, Pleasure. A kind of theology or mythology of such gods may even be developed which maintains that these "Values" have being and power apart from all human desiring; that they exercise claims upon men. Or it may be argued that nothing objective is present, that values are projections; that the basis of science is curiosity, of art the urge to make, of politics and morality the will to power. More commonly the question about the ontological status of such gods is avoided by naturalistic as well as by supernaturalistic polytheists. They move simply and uncritically from service of the lares and penates of the home to devotion to the public welfare, to participation in the worship of established religion, to concern for the increase of knowledge, to nurture of the arts.

The pluralism of the gods has its counterpart in the pluralism of self and society. What is valuable in the self is not its being in wholeness or selfhood but the activities, the knowing, creating, loving, worshiping, and directing that issue from it. It has become a bundle of functions tied together by the fibers of the body and the brain. So also the society is an assemblage of associations devoted to many partial interests, held together in meaningful unity by no common derivation from a value-center and by no loyalty to an inclusive cause.

Some thirty years ago Walter Lippmann described the situation of pluralistic modern man in words even more applicable today. "Each ideal is supreme within a sphere of its own. There is no point of reference outside which can determine the relative value of competing ideals. The modern man desires health, he desires money, he desires power, beauty, love, truth, but which of them he shall desire the most since he cannot pursue them all to their logical conclusions, he no longer has any means of deciding. His impulses are no longer part of one attitude toward life; his ideals are no longer in a hierarchy under one lordly ideal. They have become differentiated. They are free and they are incommensurable."[5] Polytheism of this sort is no peculiarly modern problem. It has appeared in every period of human history in which social faith has been shattered.

2. RADICAL MONOTHEISM

There is a third form of human faith with which we are acquainted in the West, more as hope than as datum, more perhaps as a possibility than as an actuality, yet also as an actuality that has modified at certain emergent periods our natural social faith and our polytheism. In all the times and areas of our Western history this faith has struggled with its rivals, without becoming triumphant save in passing moments and in the clarified intervals of personal existence. We look back longingly at times to some past age when, we think, confidence in the One God was the pervasive faith of men; for instance, to early Christianity, or to the church society of the Middle Ages, or to early Protestantism, or to Puritan New England, or to the pious nineteenth century. But when we study these periods we invariably find in them a mixture of the faith in the One God with social faith and polytheism; and when we examine our longings we often discover that what we yearn for is the security of the closed society with its social confidence and social loyalty. It is very questionable, despite many protestations to the contrary, despite the prevalence of self-pity among some modern men because "God is dead," that anyone has ever yearned for radical faith in the One God.

[5] *Preface to Morals*, 1929, p. 111.

We shall call this third form of faith radical monotheism.[6] We must try to describe it formally, in abstract fashion, though the form does not appear in our history or in our contemporary life otherwise than as embodied and expressed in the concreteness of communal and personal, of religious and moral existence.

For radical monotheism the value-center is neither closed society nor the principle of such a society but the principle of being itself; its reference is to no one reality among the many but to One beyond all the many, whence all the many derive their being, and by participation in which they exist. As faith, it is reliance on the source of all being for the significance of the self and of all that exists. It is the assurance that because I am, I am valued, and because you are, you are beloved, and because whatever is has being, therefore it is worthy of love. It is the confidence that whatever is, is good, because it exists as one thing among the many which all have their origin and their being, in the One—the principle of being which is also the principle of value. In Him we live and move and have our being not only as existent but as worthy of existence and worthy in existence. It is not a relation to any finite, natural or supernatural, value-center that confers value on self and some of its companions in being, but it is value relation to the One to whom all being is related. Monotheism is less than radical if it makes a distinction between the principle of being and the principle of value; so that while all being is acknowledged as absolutely dependent for existence on the One, only some beings are valued as having worth for it; or if, speaking in religious language, the Creator and the God of grace are not identified.

Radical monotheism is not in the first instance a theory about being and then a faith, as though the faith orientation toward the principle of being as value-center needed to be preceded by an ontology that established the unity of the realm of being and its source in a single power beyond it. It is not at all evident that the One beyond the many, whether made known in revelation or always present to man in hiddenness, is principle of being before it is principle of value. Believing man does not say first, "I believe in a

---

[6] The term "radical monotheism" is suggested by Rudolf Bultmann's definition of the ethics of Jesus as "radical obedience," by Erik Peterson's book *Der Monotheismus als Politisches Problem*, and by the definition liberal theology offered of prophetic religion as "ethical monotheism." Each of these definitions seem to be somewhat inaccurate yet each is helpful as a pointer.

creative principle," and then, "I believe that the principle is gracious, that is, good toward what issues from it." He rather says, "I believe in God the Father, Almighty Maker of heaven and earth." This is a primary statement, a point of departure and not a deduction. In it the principle of being is identified with the principle of value and the principle of value with the principle of being.[7] Neither is it evident, despite our intellectualist bias toward identifying ourselves with our reason, that the self is more itself as reasoning self than as faithful self, concerned about value. It is the "I" that reasons and the "I" that believes; it is present in its believing as in its reasoning. Yet the believing self must reason; there is always a reasoning in faith so that rational efforts to understand the One beyond the many are characteristic of radical monotheism. Only, the orientation of faith toward the One does not wait on the development of theory.

As faith reliance, radical monotheism depends absolutely and assuredly for the worth of the self on the same principle by which it has being; and since that principle is the same by which all things exist it accepts the value of whatever is. As faith loyalty, it is directed toward the principle and the realm of being as the cause for the sake of which it lives. Such loyalty on the one hand is claimed by the greatness and inclusiveness of the objective cause; on the other hand it is given in commitment, since loyalty is the response of a self and not the compulsive reaction of a thing. The cause also has a certain duality. On the one hand it is the principle of being itself; on the other, it is the realm of being. Whether to emphasize the one or the other may be unimportant, since the principle of being has a cause, namely, the realm of being, so that loyalty to the principle of being must include loyalty to its cause; loyalty to the realm of being, on the other hand, implies keeping faith with the principle by virtue of which it is, and is one realm.

The counterpart, then, of universal faith assurance is universal loyalty. Such universal loyalty cannot be loyalty to loyalty, as Royce would have it, but is loyalty to all existents as bound to-

---

[7] I use the terms "principle of being" and "principle of value" in distinction from the terms "highest being" and "highest value," or "Being" and "the Good," because the principle of being is not immediately to be identified with being nor the principle of value with value. As many theologians have undertaken to say, God is beyond being; they ought also to say that he is beyond value. That by reference to which all things have their value is not itself a value in the primary sense.

gether by a loyalty that is not only resident in them but transcends them. It is not only their loyalty to each other that makes them one realm of being, but the loyalty that comes from beyond them, that originates and maintains them in their particularity and their unity. Hence universal loyalty expresses itself as loyalty to each particular existent in the community of being and to the universal community. Universal loyalty does not express itself as loyalty to the loyal but to whatever is; not as reverence for the reverent but as reverence for being; not as the affirmation of world affirmers but as world affirmation. Such loyalty gives form to morality, since all moral laws and ends receive their form, though not their immediate content, from the form of faith reliance and faith loyalty. Love of the neighbor is required in every morality formed by a faith; but in polytheistic faith the neighbor is defined as the one who is near me in my interest group, when he is near me in that passing association. In henotheistic social faith my neighbor is my fellow in the closed society. Hence in both instances the counterpart of the law of neighbor-love is the requirement to hate the enemy. But in radical monotheism my neighbor is my companion in being; though he is my enemy in some less than universal context the requirement is to love him. To give to everyone his due is required in every context; but what is due to him depends on the relation in which he is known to stand.

All moral laws receive a universal form in the context of radically monotheistic faith and it is an evidence of the influence of radical faith that all our mores are haunted by the presence to the conscience of a universal form of those laws that for the most part we interpret in pluralistic and closed-society fashion. To such a universal form testimony is offered by Kant's categorical imperative, by the intuitions of universal equity and universal benevolence that Clarke and Sidgwick cannot escape, by the *prima facie* rightness of promise-keeping that Ross contends for. It is one thing to maintain that the universal form is given with reason or conscience itself; it is another thing to point out that where the universal form of moral law is acknowledged the actuality of a universal community and the claim of a universal cause have also been recognized.

The meaning of radical monotheism may be further clarified if we compare it with some of the nonradical, mixed forms of faith in which it seems to appear in disguised or broken fashion. Something like monotheism is present in henotheism at those points in personal or social life where a closed society fills the whole horizon of experience, where it is in fact not yet a closed society because everything that comes into view is a part of it. But as soon as in-group and out-group are distinguished and as soon as the contingency of the society, as not self-existent but as cast into existence, is brought to consciousness, such embryonic radical monotheism is put to the test. Though the possibility of a movement toward conscious radical monotheism may be present in such a moment, the apparently invariable process in human history at such points leads toward closed-society faith or toward polytheism or toward both.

The religion of humanity has been proclaimed by many critics of the little faiths in little gods which they find represented in the religious or national communities of their time. So far as there is protest here against forms of faith in which some men assure themselves of a special value because of their relation to a special god and in which they practice an exclusive loyalty that does not extend beyond the household of faith, we must regard such protest as movement toward universal faith assurance and faith loyalty. So Henri Bergson's critique of the defensive ethics and religion of closed societies, and his espousal of the aspiring religion and morals of open society, seem to move toward monotheism. But when he defines the open society as humanity, this aspiring religion and morality reveal themselves as merely the prelude to a new defensive and closed-society faith; so it was also with Comte's religion of humanity. Nothing human is alien to the believer in humanity and he is alien to no other human; but mankind for him remains alien in a world that contains so many other powers besides itself; and all these existents, whatever their mode of being, are alien to it. Be they worlds, or ideas, or ideals, or microbes, they derive their value only from man, and mankind's meaning depends on itself. And where does this faith find the integrating loyalty that makes the human community one? Mankind does not find the unifying center within itself any more than any individual person does. The religion of humanism, starting as protest against the doubtful assurance and the partial loyalties of closed societies, ends with an enlarged but yet dubious and partial closed-society faith. It remains a kind of henotheism.

Again naturalism, insofar as it expresses a faith, as it often does, is intelligible to us as a movement of protest against exclusive loyalties and dubious assurances of value. Most frequently the faith it seeks to live by is humanistic but sometimes it sees man as significant because of his participation in a more than human community, the world of nature. Whether this reality whence he derives his being is regarded as implicitly purposive, moving toward unspecified good ends in wonderful progression, or whether it be regarded aesthetically as marvellous in its unity of the diverse, or whether it be otherwise conceived as unified, still it is from nature that man derives his meaning. Nothing natural is alien to him and he is alien to nothing natural. Moreover, nature becomes an object of loyalty, a cause. To understand nature through science, not because its forces can so be made serviceable to man, but because nature is there and is remarkable; to find out its "laws" and willingly to accept and conform to them; to make explicit its implicit purposes—this becomes man's purpose in naturalistic faith. As a faith it is more inclusive than even humanism. But it is also a closed-society faith and not a radical monotheism. Being is greater in extent than nature as is indicated by the place naturalism must accord to ideals that attract and compel men, which, it believes, somehow emerge out of nature yet are not actual in it.[8] In such naturalism the conflict of radical monotheism with henotheism comes to appearance, yet naturalism remains henotheistic in its refusal even to entertain the possibility that there are provinces of being not accessible to its special methods of understanding, in its reduction of all value to value-in-relation-to-nature. Into its faith loyalty an element of polytheism also intrudes, expressed in the manifoldness of ideals to be served.

More inclusive than humanism, less so than naturalism, is Albert Schweitzer's faith, so far as this is expressed in his writings rather than in his action; for in this case the confession of a life lived is greater than the confession in words. "Reverence for life" means that life is the value-center; whatever lives is good and to be reverenced because it participates in life and is the creation of life. Life is the value-center rather than the value; living beings call forth reverence because they are functions of the will-to-live. Reverence for life is also the expression of a loyalty that goes out to the whole realm of the living and every member of it. The man who has consciously found his ground in the unconscious will-to-live "feels a

[8] See for instance John Dewey's *A Common Faith*, 1934, esp. Chap. II. In writing this section I have also had in mind the unacknowledged role that the ideal of human liberty plays in Spinoza's *Ethics*.

compulsion," writes Schweitzer, "to give to every will-to-live the same reverence for life that he gives to his own. He experiences that other life in his own. He accepts as being good: to preserve life, to promote life, to raise to its highest value life which is capable of development; and as being evil: to destroy life, to injure life, to repress life which is capable of development. This is the absolute, fundamental principle of the moral."[9] One notes the protest in Schweitzer's assertion of faith against all closed systems, including humanism. But he is not asserting a radically monotheistic faith. This is the henotheism of the community of the living which excludes from the realm of value all that is not alive; and from the sphere of loyalty all beings that are not endowed with that biological will-to-live I find within myself. A radical monotheism would include reverence for the dead, and that not simply because they were once alive; it would include also reverence for beings, inorganic perhaps, perhaps ideal, that though not living claim the wondering and not exploitative attention of us other creatures that have the will-to-live.

All such ways of faith seem, at least as protests, to be movements in the direction of radical monotheism. Yet they all fall short of the radical expression; each excludes some realm of being from the sphere of value; each is claimed by a cause less inclusive than the realm of being in its wholeness.

Radical monotheism dethrones all absolutes short of the principle of being itself. At the same time it reverences every relative existent. Its two great mottoes are: "I am the Lord thy God; thou shalt have no other gods before me" and "Whatever is, is good."

[9] *Out of My Life and Thought*, 1933, pp. 186-88.

Radical Faith—Incarnate and Revealed in History

RADICAL monotheism, as I have tried to define it, is a form of human faith, that is, of the confidence and fidelity without which men do not live. It may, but need not, be expressed in verbalized beliefs. When the confidence is so put into words the resultant assertion is not that there is a God but that Being is God, or, better, that the principle of being, the source of all things and the power by which they exist, is good, as good for them and good to them. It is relied upon to give and conserve worth to all that issues from it. What otherwise, in distrust and suspicion, is regarded as fate or destiny or blind will or chance is now trusted. It is God. As loyalty such radical faith is decision for and commitment to the One beyond all the many as head and center of the realm of being; its cause, the universe of being, elicits and requires fidelity. So for faith the kingdom of God is both the rule that is trusted and the realm to which loyalty is given. To say that this faith acknowledges whatever is to be good is not to say, of course, that for it whatever is, is right. In their relations to each other and to their principle these many beings in the realm of being are often wrong and grievously so. They are enemies to each other as often as friends; but even enemies are entitled to loyalty as fellow citizens of the realm of being.

Radical monotheism of this sort has struggled continuously in Western religion as in the whole of Western culture with the other forms of faith.[1] Officially our religious institutions and rites

[1] In confining the ensuing discussion to Western culture I do not wish to imply that radical monotheism has emerged nowhere else. The question

are monotheistic; actually we can discern in them, without much more than a casual glance, many tendencies toward polytheism and especially toward henotheistic or social faith. On the other hand the wrestle of radical faith with its rivals is manifest in other areas of our culture besides religion. Hence the common theme of this and the following chapters must be "Monotheism and Western culture" rather than "Religious faith and Western culture." Hence also we shall need to deal with religion as one of the spheres of human activity in which the struggle of the faiths is continuous.

1. The Incarnation of Radical Faith

The emergence of radical monotheism in the West took place, we may say, at a time prior to the now conventional separation of our cultural activities into such domains as the religious, the political, the scientific, the economic, and the aesthetic. Or we must say, that insofar as these differentiations were already present the emergence of radical monotheism challenged the pluralistic faith which tended to divide them sharply from each other as independent provinces. It is difficult to classify Moses as a religious, a political, or an ethical figure or to designate the movement that began with him by one of these terms. He was a prophet and a chief and a lawgiver; perhaps also a poet. It is only by virtue of relatively late developments and conventions that we put him in the category of founders of religion rather than of fathers of nations or of the solons of constitutional societies. Similarly when we attend to later appearances in the history of the radical faith we find that we are dealing with men and movements that are called religious only by a convention which somewhat falsifies their concern and effect. Israel's great prophets were legal reformers, ethical seers, purifiers of religious cults, theological critics, political advisers, poets, perhaps originators of a new literary style or even exponents of new types of aesthetic sensibility. To their contemporaries they often seemed antireligious, and indeed some of them had little use for religious ritual or for the official clergy. So also Jesus Christ, who mediated the radical faith to folk whom

---

of the relation of this form of faith to the monisms of the East is left aside partly because I am not prepared by intimate knowledge to explore it, partly because the present situation seems to require first of all critical self-knowledge on the part of Western man if his encounters with the East are to be fruitful.

Moses and the prophets did not reach, seems out of place in the classification of founders of religion. He appeared as a strange figure who constituted both threat and promise to men in their political, economic, and moral existence as well as in their religion. Again the great medieval synthesis and the sixteenth-century Reformation were events in the total social culture, not so much because a change in religion affected the rest of human action as because a newly emergent confidence and new decisions of loyalty affected all life. In such moments men's natural pluralism and social narcissism, together with their deep distrust of existence, were overcome for at least a moment and the consequences became evident in all spheres of activity.

We may use the theological word "incarnation" in speaking of the coming of radically monotheistic faith into our history, meaning by it the concrete expression in a total human life of radical trust in the One and of universal loyalty to the realm of being. One way of describing the difference between the tendencies toward monotheism in Greek philosophy and the appearance of monotheistic faith in the life of the Hebrews is to say that in the former monotheism, so far as it was present, was an element in a movement of thought while in the latter it was an element in total personal and communal life. In Greece we encounter the *idea* of the One beyond all the many and perhaps an effort to permeate the whole activity of reason with universal confidence and loyalty. But this monistic tendency in thought had a kind of epiphenomenal existence in a society that lived by social faith with its concrete expression and representation in the life of the *polis* or by polytheism, so closely related to the sensed objects of desire and love. Hence in Greece the conflict of monotheism with its rivals is part of the history of thought. Among the Hebrews, however, it is a part of the history of domestic and political, of national and international, of commercial and religious activities. The radical faith becomes incarnate in this sense in Israel. This is not to say that it is wholly or unambiguously incarnate there, for the history of that people is filled with accounts of strife between radical and social faith. But monotheism is expressed in all activities and the conflict about it takes place in connection with each activity. The observance of the Sabbath day, the using of weights and measures in the market place, the attitude toward the unfortunate, the making of treaties with other nations—all involve faith, the practice of

trust and of loyalty; and in connection with each the problem of
the form of faith arises. It is not enough to say that Israel's religion is ethical and its ethics religious nor that its religion is one
of ethical monotheism. Such definitions could be offered only
by men who believed with Kant that monistic ethical principles
are accessible to men simply as rational beings. They did not seem
to realize that ethics itself is always involved in conflicts of faith.
In ethics as in religion the struggle in Israel was one between radical
faith in the principle of being and social faith with its reference
to the principle of the society as center of value and as cause.

One way of describing the incarnate character of radical faith in
the life of Israel is to say that for this people all human relations were
transformed into covenant relations. Promise-making and promise-
keeping were the essential elements in every connection between
persons. Religion became such a matter of covenant. Whatever
the natural connections might be between creator and creature
or between the god of the fathers and the latter's children, these
were transformed into faith relations when the creator and the
god of the fathers committed himself by a promise to maintain
and save the people and when they in turn responded with an
oath of allegiance to him. Now religious observance became fundamentally an affair of promise-keeping, or of keeping faith, in
carrying on covenanted practices of worship and sacrifice. Domestic,
commercial, and political relations were no less covenantal in
character. The family, with all its natural basis in sex and parental
love, was now given a subfoundation as it were in promise and the
keeping of faith between husbands and wives, parents and children.
The natural kinship of tribes having a common ancestry or language was in part replaced, in part reinforced, by the structure of
covenant; the political tie was less one of the love of one's own
kind or of the native soil than of explicit fidelity in keeping the
oath of a citizen. Man was understood, in this whole context,
as Martin Buber has pointed out, not first of all as rational animal
but as promise-making, promise-keeping, promise-breaking being,
as man of faith. All life was permeated by the faith in the fundamental covenant between God and man and in every activity some
phase of that covenant was re-enacted. Faith as confidence in the
One and as loyalty to the universe of being was ingredient in every
action and relation. Very often, to be sure, it was encountered
in its negative forms of distrust and disloyalty, which are to positive

faith as minus 1, not 0, is to plus 1, or as error, not ignorance, is to the life of reason.

Jesus Christ represents the incarnation of radical faith to an even greater extent than Israel. The greatness of his confidence in the Lord of heaven and earth as fatherly in goodness toward all creatures, the consistency of his loyalty to the realm of being, seem unqualified by distrust or by competing loyalty. The faith is expressed in acts of healing as well as in teaching, in his intrepretation of the historic moment in which he lives and in the leadership he seeks to give to his people, in his relations to national enemies and to the morally rejected. His confidence and his fidelity are those of a son of God—the most descriptive term which Christians apply to him as they contemplate the faith of their Lord. The word of God as God's oath of fidelity became flesh in him in this sense that he was a man who single-mindedly accepted the assurance that the Lord of heaven and earth was wholly faithful to him and to all creatures, and who in response gave wholehearted loyalty to the realm of being.

2. Revelation and Faith

The counterpart of those incarnations of radical faith to which we trace the rise of monotheism in the West is revelation. Though the word is used with other meanings in other contexts, in this context revelation specifies those events in which radical faith was elicited. In relation to faith, revelation does not mean the impartation of certain truths, for propositions do not in themselves establish confidence or challenge to loyalty. The event that calls forth faith as confidence is a demonstration of loyalty and the event that calls forth faith as loyalty is some disclosure of a cause.

Professor Etienne Gilson describes the critical event in which the Western understanding of God was established in the following fashion: "In order to know what God is, Moses turns to God. He asks his name, and straightway comes the answer: *Ego sum qui sum, Ait: sic dices filiis Israel: qui est misit me ad vos.* (Exodus III, 14.) No hint of metaphysics, but God speaks, *causa finita est,* and Exodus lays down the principle from which henceforth the whole of Christian philosophy will be suspended. From this moment it is understood once and for all that the proper name of God is Being and that . . . this name denotes His very essence."[2] This is well

---

[2] *The Spirit of Medieval Philosophy,* 1936, p. 51.

said, but we need to point to some other elements in the revelation that elicits faith. One of these is the statement in the Exodus narrative preceding God's identification of himself as "I am that I am": "I am the God of your father, the God of Abraham, the God of Isaac, and the God of Jacob. . . . I have seen the affliction of my people . . . and have heard their cry . . . and I have come down to deliver them." The other is Moses' commissioning in the same moment to be God's agent in the liberation. Insofar as the Exodus story describes a revelatory event three notes at least are combined in it: (1) God is nothing less than being; (2) being is God, namely, valuer and savior; (3) Moses is challenged to choose God's cause as his own.[3]

When the prophets of the Old Testament speak of revelation or of the word of God that came to them the same three notes occur. Salvation, to be sure, does not mean deliverance from external oppression in all cases; more frequently it appears in its harsher forms as judgment and discipline that re-order a world of disloyalties. Yet in that case it may be even more evident that the principle of being is the principle of worth and that what is elicited in revelation is the confidence that being can be relied upon to maintain as well as give value in a universe of interdependent values.

When Christians refer to Jesus Christ as the revelation of God they do not or ought not have less than the three notes of faith in mind, the note that the valuing, saving power in the world is the principle of being itself; that the ultimate principle of being gives and maintains and re-establishes worth; that they have been called upon to make the cause of that God their cause. It is of course a fact that Christians, like Jews, often have other things in mind when they speak of revelation; they may refer to some disclosure of a private God; or to some event that has elicited confidence without challenging loyalty; or to a religious event that

---

[3] Not too much weight must be rested on this Exodus passage as though it contained the essence of revelation. Both the figure of Moses and the meaning of the burning bush narrative, especially of the "I am" statement, have been obscured and rendered uncertain rather than clarified by historical research and criticism. Perhaps radical monotheism did not appear in history until much later than the period to which the passage refers. But when it appeared—indubitably in the case of Second Isaiah—the motifs here discovered in the Exodus passage were sounded. Cf. Gerhard von Rad, *Theologie des Alten Testamentes*, 1958; vol. I, pp. 182 ff., 209-11 (English translation to be published in 1961).

established a certain form of worship. Yet insofar as the Christ event elicits radical faith it is seen as demonstration of Being's loyalty to all beings and as call to decisive choice of God's universal cause.

Of such revelatory events to which we trace the emergence of the radical faith in the West we can say what we have said of faith itself—namely, that they did not occur in a peculiarly religious sphere of human action and interest. The events were not mystic visions or ecstatic experiences in which men were transported out of their daily world; they were not answers to human cries for help directed to supernatural powers; they were not peculiarly encounters with the holy. The revelatory moments occurred in the midst of political struggles, of national and cultural crises. As they were acknowledged by a faith that was incarnate in a total human life so they were experienced as demonstrations of a presence that was present in every situation.

3. FAITH IN THE PERSON

We may approach the problem of distinguishing between what in our modern world we call religious convictions and this more than religious confidence, defined as radical faith, by attending to the relation of such confidence to the life of selves. Instead of saying that radical faith emerged in the West as incarnate in total life, prior to or beyond all divisions of activities into separate provinces, we might say that it emerged as an attitude of selves who remained true to themselves in all their roles and offices. Instead of saying that the moments in which such faith was elicited were those in which the loyalty of the principle of being to the realm of being was demonstrated, we might say less abstractly that they were moments in which the ultimate made itself known as faithful self.

In the statement in Exodus to which we have previously referred—"Say to the children of Israel 'I am has sent me'"—the word "I" is as startling as the word "am." If, following Professor Gilson, we say that "from this moment it is understood once and for all that the proper name of God is Being," we ought to follow it with the observation that from this moment it is also acknowledged once and for all that the principle of Being is the First Person. Of course such an avowal raises a host of problems about tendencies toward anthropomorphism in our understanding of our

ultimate environment. Yet if the cornerstone of Christian philosophy is the conviction that "there is but one God and this God is
Being," the cornerstone of Christian as of Jewish and all radical
monotheist confidence and loyalty is that the one God who is
Being is an "I," or like an "I," who is faithful as only selves are
faithful.

To our conceptualizing mind, though we count ourselves believers in the One, this personal concreteness is always something
of a scandal, and that not only because we foresee dangers of con-
structing for ourselves an idol made in our human image. When
we try to think and speak intelligibly and rationally, from mind to
mind, we abjure the use of personal pronouns, of "I" and "Thou."
Then we speak of ideas rather than of persons, of forms and laws
rather than of you and me and him. Amidst the confusion of our
encounters with the environing world of realities we seek understanding by looking for recurrent patterns of behavior or enduring
structures or permanent relations or abstract universals. We try to
unify our experiences and our thoughts about them with the aid of
impersonal symbols, among which mathematical symbols seem
the least personal, most orderly, manageable, and unambiguous.
When we reason practically as moral beings we try to deal with
ideals to be actualized, with laws to be obeyed, and with abstract
values to be honored or chosen. When we reason as theologians
we undertake to define *ideas* of God, *forms* of faith, *notions* of the
soul, *theories* of salvation. To reason so oriented and employing
such instruments there is something animistic, prelogical, or mythological in all speech and thinking that use personal pronouns as
ultimate terms of reference.

Yet there is something in our human existence, in our world,
with our companions and in ourselves that cannot be denied yet
cannot be understood with the aid of impersonal categories. All
our experiencing and experimenting, our thinking and communicating goes on within a complex interaction of irreducible "I's" and
"You's." Our efforts to think depersonalized, logical thoughts and
to speak from common reason to common reason, about experience
available to any sensing, thoughtful being are still the efforts
of thinking selves who acknowledge the presence of other thinking
selves. No matter how much we concentrate on common objects,
this is the concentration of subjects who acknowledge the presence
of other subjects, of thinkers rather than thoughts, experiencers

rather than the experienced. Yet in attending to faith we are aware of something more important than the subjectivity of selves. We take for granted or acknowledge in all our thinking and communicating the presence of selves as loyal or disloyal, trusting or distrusting beings and are aware of the great problem of interpersonal truth. In the midst of seeking true understanding of objects and in our efforts to formulate it accurately we note that truth and untruth are present also as relations between selves. When we try to develop true theories we think of truth as a relationship between such theories and the objective states to which they refer; yet we formulate and communicate such truths in the interpersonal situation in which truth and falsehood are present between selves who can lie to each other or be loyal. They can under circumstances be very objective and accurate with the intention of deceiving companions. Or, in another familiar situation, the technically trained man seeking to be truthful to an untrained friend strains his scientific conscience because what he must say so as not to deceive does not adequately correspond to the facts. The problems we face in this region are not those of the difference between objective and subjective truth or between what is universally true and what is true for me. They are rather those of impersonal and personal truth, between the truth that is the opposite of error or ignorance and the truth that is antithesis to lie or deception.

Now the first sort of truth which is a relation of thought to things is inseparable from the second which is a relation of a self to selves. We often abstract the one from the other, but in any situation in which objective truth is considered interpersonal truth is also involved. No scientific inquiry or treatise, no logical analysis, as well as no poem or political address, but what brings before us a self who in addition to being a thought-ful being dealing with objects is a faith-ful being to be trusted or distrusted as truthful or untruthful toward other selves. Liable to error as a subject dealing with objects, he is also liable to deception as self dealing with selves; able to know the truth about things he is at the same time able to keep truth with companions or deceive them.

To say that God makes himself known as First Person is to say that revelation means less the disclosure of the essence of objective being to minds than the demonstration to selves of faithful, truthful being. What we try to point to with the aid of conceptual terms as principle of being or as the One beyond the many is acknowledged by selves as "Thou." The integrity that is before them here is the oneness of a self; it is the faithfulness that keeps promises, is indefectibly loyal, is truthful in freedom. God is stedfast self, keeping his word, "faithful in all his doings and just in all his ways." This principle of personlike integrity is fundamental in a revelation that is an event which elicits the confidence of selves in their ultimate environment and calls upon them as free selves to decide for the universal cause.

As revelation so considered means the event in which the ultimate unity is disclosed as personal or faithful, so the human response to such revelation is the development of integrated selfhood. Such integration in the presence of the faithful One is in part an affair of reasoning faith. When we reason as depersonalized public minds we look for recurrent patterns and laws in many events so that we can say in the midst of initially novel experiences, "There it is again"; but reasoning faith looks for the presence of one faithful person in the multiplicity of the events that happen to the self and learns to say "There he is again." In the story of Biblical faith the revelation of the First Person was the beginning of a process of coherent reasoning in faith for which no event in nature or in social history could be dismissed as accidental, arbitrary, unintelligible, or disconnected, as product of some independent power. No plague, no drought, no invasion, no sparrow's fall occurred apart from the faithful will of the One. Confidence in cosmic faithfulness held to the assurance that there was one self-consistent intention in apparent evil as well as in apparent good though how it was present often remained unfathomed. His ways were not man's ways, nor his thoughts man's thoughts; reasoning faith struggled to overcome anthropomorphism. It became clear that the righteousness of God was not like human justice. The suffering of the innocent, the prosperity of the wicked, brought faith to the edge of despair. But the postulate that God is faithful remained after every hypothesis about the mode of his faithfulness had broken down, as is magnificently illustrated in the book of Job. How a new idea of divine righteousness gave new direction to the life of faith is greatly described in Paul's letter to the Romans.

All this unified and unifying reasoning we must remember is primarily practical reasoning. It is the effort to understand on the part of selves who are deciding how to act in response to action upon them, not for the sake of surviving nor for the sake of maintaining some partial cause but as loyal to the inclusive cause. To translate such practical reasoning into depersonalized speculative explanations of events that call for no practical decision is always perilous to the practical reason itself, no less than it is unsatisfactory to the theoretic mind. Hence the problem of the integrity of the self arises before us in a new form as we confront this duality which is not that of faith and reason but of reasoning faith and reasoning in abstraction from confidence and loyalty. But we cannot approach the solution of that problem by ignoring the self that lives in faith and moves either toward integrity or toward irrational multiplicity in its practical reasoning.

Integration of the self in the presence of the First Person is not only an affair of the practical understanding of all events that happen to the self or its community. The elicited trust and loyalty of radical monotheism express themselves in the positive response to such events. The radical faith becomes incarnate insofar as every reaction to every event becomes a response in loyalty and confidence to the One who is present in all such events. The First Person encountered in the temple is also the First Person encountered in the political arena, or in the market place, or among the hungry and plague-ridden. No action directed toward human companions or toward other nations or toward animals but is also directed toward the One who is their creator and savior. The consistent ethics of radical faith is not constituted by the attachment of certain ethical rules to religious beliefs but by the requirement and the empowerment to consistent action in all realms and offices in which the self acts. Insofar as the confidence in the One and loyalty to his realm is present the self cannot, in moving from one society to another, accept in succession varying codes of conduct; the One is present in every place and all society is one. It cannot remain internally divided as it pursues now one interest, now another, for all its loves are drawn together toward him and his realm.

Radical faith, therefore, is either expressed by the self in all its roles and relations, or is not expressed at all. It is either revealed to and incarnate in the total human life or it does not exist. If it is present it manifests itself in religion as well as elsewhere. But in religion as in other human actions monotheistic faith is in constant conflict with our natural henotheism and our despairing polytheism.

IV

Radical Monotheism and Western Religion

How has radically monotheistic faith affected religion in the West? The question may seem meaningless if we come to our subject with the conventional view according to which the word "religion" is the name of a genus of which our "organized religions" —Christianity and Judaism—are special examples; according to which also each such representative "religion" is a unitary system. For this view the Western "organized religions" are monotheistic while elsewhere in the world there are henotheistic or polytheistic religions. Further, according to the convention, polytheism and henotheism as types of faith may flourish in other areas of our Western culture, but our religions are by definition exempt from invasion by them.

Such a view seems confused and to rest upon a set of unanalyzed assumptions. For it, "religion" means both piety—personal relations to divine powers—and also the great historic combinations of doctrine, ritual, organization, and common ethos that we encounter in Christianity, Judaism, Mohammedanism, Buddhism, Confucianism, Taoism, Shintoism, etc. But it is well-known that in these historic and communal movements we meet much that is not religion in the sense of piety. Further, every effort to define the genus "religion," of which the "religions" are thought to be examples, results either in great vagueness or in general statements that should make it necessary to include under the head of religion schools of philosophy such as Platonism, Stoicism, and Epicureanism, and political movements such as Marxism and the nationalisms.

Again the assumption that Christianity and Judaism are highly

49

unitary systems, essentially monotheistic in their faith, is subject to many questions, if by Judaism and Christianity we mean the communities that call themselves by these names and not some idea of "true Christianity" or "true Judaism." If we look at these "organized religions" as they present themselves to us in their present-day social forms, practices and beliefs, as well as in their historical development, it is difficult to regard them as representative of one idea or attitude or as highly systematic in character or as derivative from one source. They are not like plants that have grown out of a single seed but more like forests with trees and undergrowth of many origins. They are not like persons with definable bodies, minds, and intentions. Their doctrines and thoughts have an even more manifold origin than those of any individual and are brought into coherent order far less frequently than happens in the case of persons. They are movements in human history; they are more or less close-knit communities. In them we encounter drives, needs, feelings, traditions, doctrines, and practices which, though derivative from many sources, have been brought more or less under the influence of certain powerful convictions or attracted toward certain magnetic centers. The law of Moses and the person of Jesus Christ, for instance, have become transforming powers and organizing principles in a common life whose manifold activities, world-views, and interests are not directly derivative from these persons or historic occasions. But the unity we find in them is never complete, least of all, one is tempted to say, have they achieved a unity in monotheistic faith as trust in the One and loyalty to his cause.

In order that we may avoid the confusions and questionable assumptions in which we would find ourselves involved if we tried to operate with the categories of the conventional view we shall abstain from every effort to deal with "religion and the religions" in the broad sense and shall try to further understanding of our culture by asking the more specific questions: How has monotheistic faith affected human religion as piety? And how has the issue of monotheism and polytheism come to appearance in the "organized religions" of Judaism and Christianity?

1. The Conversion of Reverence and Prayer

One element in human experience that is encountered in advanced as well as in naïve piety is the sense or idea of the

Holy. To some theologians, as well as to some psychologists of religion, this sense or idea seems to be the fundamental characteristic or the distinguishing mark of the religious as contrasted with the ethical, the aesthetic, or the intellectual activities of the human mind or spirit. By the sense of the holy they mean that peculiar feeling of awe and reverence which seems to be mainly a kind of combination of fear and attraction but which contains other affective elements also. The "idea of the holy" is the projected idea or the objective presence in things of majestic, strange and other-worldly, fearsome and fascinating, "numinous" power before which men experience the feeling of awe. The sense and idea of the holy are expressed in such Biblical statements as Job's, "I had heard of thee by the hearing of the ear, but now my eye sees thee; therefore I despise myself, and repent in dust and ashes"; or in Isaiah's "Woe is me! For I am lost; for I am a man of unclean lips, and I dwell in the midst of a people of unclean lips; for my eyes have seen the King, the Lord of hosts!" We encounter the holy in primitive religion where the terms "mana," "orenda," and the like refer not to personal deities but to strange power subjectively experienced in tremor and fascination, in horror and ecstasy. The sense of the holy is present in the philosopher's awe before the starry heavens and the moral law within. It is present also in the sense of sin experienced not as moral guilt because of the transgression of laws but as "uncleanness," "pollution," and profaneness.[1]

The sense of the holy is diffuse; in itself it is not polytheistic, henotheistic, or monotheistic. But by means of social ritual, doctrine, and tradition it is organized and directed toward certain objects or events. In this process of organization the form of faith is very influential. Polytheism with its many centers of values and many causes of devotion attaches holiness to certain natural objects or events while others remain common and unexciting; mountains may become objects of awe rather than be merely frightening; storms may lose their numinous character as a special polytheistic tradition is established. For the most part contemporary polytheism finds and experiences mysterious sublimity in the works of men—in great music, in the breath-taking spans of great bridges, in soaring towers. In social henotheism the sense of the holy is directed through rite and doctrine toward the symbols of the closed society.

[1] See especially Rudolf Otto, *The Idea of the Holy.*

The sacredness of some natural objects—of green islands, rivers, of "woods and templed hills"—is derivative from the holiness of the society that identifies with itself the land it inhabits and which it has hallowed in historic moments of tragedy or exaltation. Divinity hedges about the kings who symbolize the social continuity, unity, and power, so that awe and reverence, the sense of the sublime and mysterious, are experienced in rites enacted at coronations and every royal appearance. Flags become sacred objects to be treated with holy fear. The display of social power in military reviews excites the feeling of grandeur and glory as well as of tremor. The documents of national history become sacred books, their phrases holy words, more evocative of reverent emotions than of interpretative ideas. The closed society may, of course, be a church rather than a city or a nation. Then other numinous symbols of the social unity become the occasion for the expression of awe. But in all such instances the sense of the holy has been channeled and directed by a henotheistic form of faith.

Radical monotheism organizes the sense of the holy in another fashion. Its first effect is the consistent secularization of all those symbolic objects that polytheism and henotheism meet with sacred fear and joy. The antireligious strain found in the prophets of the radical faith is largely explicable as attack not on religious emotion itself but on the systematization of that emotion by nonmonotheistic forms of faith. When the principle of being is God—i.e., the object of trust and loyalty—then he alone is holy and ultimate sacredness must be denied to any special being. No special places, times, persons, or communities are more representative of the One than any others are. No sacred groves or temples, no hallowed kings or priests, no festival days, no chosen communities are particularly representative of Him in whom all things live and move and have their being. A Puritan iconoclasm has ever accompanied the rise of radical faith.

The counterpart of this secularization, however, is the sanctification of all things. Now every day is the day that the Lord has made; every nation is a holy people called by him into existence in its place and time and to his glory; every person is sacred, made in his image and likeness; every living thing, on earth, in the heavens, and in the waters is his creation and points in its existence toward him; the whole earth is filled with his glory; the infinity of space is his temple where all creation is summoned to silence before him. Here is the basis then not only of a transformed ethics, founded on the recognition that whatever is, is good, but of transformed piety or religion, founded on the realization that every being is holy.

How difficult the monotheistic reorganization of the sense of the holy is, the history of Western organized religion makes plain. In it we encounter ever new efforts to draw some new line of division between the holy and the profane. A holy church is separated from a secular world; a sacred priesthood from an un-hallowed laity; a holy history of salvation from the unsanctified course of human events; the sacredness of human personality, or of life, is maintained along with the acceptance of a purely utilitarian valuation of animal existence or of nonliving being. The secular aspects of holy books, churches, and histories are denied; the holiness of the secular is unrealized. Organized religion often seems to co-operate with other institutions in the attempt to give a purely utilitarian evaluation to natural goods, physical life, political activity, and family existence. In the history of Western organized religion we cannot discern a progressive movement toward universal secularization accompanying universal sanctification of being, but only ever new reformations tending in that direction, followed by renewed lapses into the bifurcation of the holy and the profane. Perhaps it is impossible insofar as the sense of the holy is emotional in character to order it completely by the principle of monotheistic faith. Yet faith, as confidence and loyalty, seeks to rise above the emotional level and to resolve that even if the feeling of the holy is not experienced, nevertheless since all things are holy because of their relations to the holy One they must be so respected; and that nothing—whatever emotion man experiences —is deserving of the unqualified reverence which is due only to the One.

A second element encountered in all piety, which, like the idea of the holy, is regarded by some theologians and philosophers as the central feature of the religious life, is prayer for superhuman help, arising out of man's anxiety and peril. In all his physical and spiritual adversities, in all his wakeful care for threatened companions and beloved communities, man cries out to angels and ministers of grace for defense. The prayer for superhuman aid doubtless rises out of levels of the psychic life that lie deeper than consciousness; in despair men even cry out to powers in whose presence they do not consciously believe. Like the sense of the holy the activity of prayer seems basically diffuse. The powers to which prayers are directed, like those whose presence is felt in the experience of the holy, are identified and named only as religion is given structure, especially by faith. In polytheism we learn to address our supplications to the spirits that preside over, or that are resident within, the enterprises or concerns in which we experience our dangers. In anxiety for ourselves or our families we call upon our fathers and the gods of our fathers, or on the spirits of the dead who were mighty in our infancy. If error and lie assail us we invoke the spirit and the power of truth on which we rely to maintain itself and its cause. If injustice prevails we pray not only for justice but to the spirit or power of justice to manifest itself again. In henotheism we learn to direct our prayers to the god of our society, the god of our social fathers, as not only the defender of the community but of every member of it also, and we invoke the aid of martyrs, heroes, and saints who made this social cause their own.

Radical monotheism does not teach men to pray but how to pray to the One, how so to make supplications and intercessions that they are made in confidence in him and are coherent with his cause. Though the prayers be for food and for forgiveness they are now set within the context of prayer for the doing of his will and the coming of his kingdom; though they are petitions for the self they are offered in the midst of intercession for every being in need of aid and succor. In radical faith men learn to pray in confidence and quietness without frantic efforts to appease the power whence life and death both issue; they learn to pray to the One who cares for all as though they were but one and for each one as though he were all; they learn to pray as those who expect a change of mind less in the One on whom they call than in themselves. Nothing in man's natural prayer religion is denied by the radical faith; every part of it is reoriented and reorganized.

When we consider the private and institutional prayer practices of Western organized religion we cannot speak with assurance of the transformation of man's prayer life by monotheistic faith as though this reorganization were an accomplished fact. Within the sphere of Western religion as well as elsewhere prayer seems often to remain unformed or unreformed. Magic uses of incantations and supplications continue among us. The god to whom prayers are addressed is not infrequently identified with the group deity whose special concern is with Christians or Jews and whose cause is identified with their cause more than theirs is with his. Unrepentant petitions for infidels and heretics, for countries and churches in conflict with others, the praise and defense of prayer itself: these are among the symptoms of the continuation of a religion of supplication uncriticized and unreorganized by faith in the One.

Other elements in the complex phenomenon we call religion could be taken into consideration in our analysis of the role of monotheistic faith in religious life. Besides the sense of the holy and the need for superhuman aid we encounter in religion the desire for ecstasy, for transport out of the ordinary round of routine existence into realms of wonder, of increased sensitivity, of enlarged views, of freedom from constraint, of "surprises by joy." Religion as piety is also an affair of rites of expiation and of celebration; and of doctrines and beliefs that set forth men's fundamental sense of orientation in their universe. The specific ways in which the desire for ecstasy is satisfied or denied, in public rites and in private practices of mystic devotion, are influenced by a number of factors —the historic tradition of a religious society, the total culture in which it participates, the doctrines taught. But the form of faith, of confidence and loyalty, also determines these ways and the meanings that are attached to them. The hymns that are sung, the sacraments that are administered and interpreted, the symbolism presented in color and sound express more than the faith. But all these things receive their specific form in part from the particular type of confidence and loyalty that prevails.

So it is with doctrines that set forth, more or less literally, more or less poetically, men's orientation in nature, in time and history and in what lies beyond their limits, in supernature, supertime, and superhistory. These doctrines do not issue from the confidence and loyalty in the many or the One. In Christianity the general doctrines of creation, of fall, and of redemption seem to have manifold sources in historic revelations, in reasoning, in imagination and wonder, in experiences of evil and of good. But they are formed by the form of faith. The doctrine of redemption, for instance, may be stated in the context of confidence in the principle of being and of loyalty to all the realm of being. So it was set forth by Paul when he saw the whole creation waiting "with eager longing for the revealing of the sons of God; for the creation was subjected to futility, not of its own will but by the will of him who subjected it in hope; because the creation itself will be set free from its bondage to decay and obtain the glorious liberty of the children of God" (Rom. 8:19-21). But it may also be set forth within the context of a henotheistic faith that reserves redemption to men, or to the few devotees of a god whose cause excludes most of the realm of being.

The reorganization and transformation of such highly complex religion by faith in the One never seems to be complete in any individual or any institution. It never remains stable. No reformation remains reformed; no catholic church remains all-inclusive. The One beyond the many is confused again and again with one of the many. The God in whose presence we acknowledge our world to be one, and commit ourselves in loyalty to being, is confused again in distrust and disloyalty, in ignorance and error, with the god who is the principle or the collective representation of the closed society of some beings, or otherwise, is a spirit immanent in some special activities only. The struggle of the radical faith with its rivals is no less present in the realm of piety than it is within the spheres of other human activities and attitudes.

2. Radical Faith in "Organized Religion"

When we turn from the question about monotheistic faith in relation to religion as piety to the question about the relation of that faith to the "organized religions" in the West—Judaism and Christianity—two observations force themselves upon us: first, the struggle for monotheism has been continuous in the history of these societies and is at present being carried on in them; secondly, though we call Judaism and Christianity "religions" they are not only concerned with religion as personal or communal piety but seem to be efforts at the incarnation of monotheistic faith in total life. These two facts seem interrelated but we must attempt to construct the whole picture by attending to each one in turn.

Those of us who call ourselves Christians have been prone to to see the mote of particularism in our Israelite brother's eye while disregarding the plank in our own. The God worshiped by Israel, we note, was almost always somewhat an Israelite god. Israel, we tend to say, thinking of itself as a chosen nation, meant when it spoke of its election that it had been especially favored by a deity who was more the Holy One of Israel than the Lord of heaven and earth. Hence it tended to believe that it had been endowed with special privileges more than charged with special responsibilities. So it thought of itself as the holy nation in such fashion that there was no access to God except through membership in its community. While it is strange that Christians should charge Jews with this error as though it were peculiarly Jewish, it does seem clear from any study of the Hebrew Scriptures that the history of Israel is marked by an almost continuous struggle between social henotheism and radical monotheism.

The tension between a faith directed toward the Holy One of Israel and the Lord of heaven and earth appears not only in the antithesis between the monotheistic books of eighth-century prophets and such praises of a tribal deity as one encounters in a Song of Deborah, but it also runs through the writings of the prophets themselves and appears in the Psalms. It seems to be present in the story of God's revelation of himself to Moses as God of the fathers and as "I am that I am." Evolutionary theory saw in the development of Israelite religion only upward movement from henotheism to monotheism; but the movement from Second Isaiah to Ezra and Nehemiah seems to run in the opposite direction. Furthermore, the two faiths do not appear only in succession but seem to be present in all periods and to be in conflict with each other at all times. The tension is probably present, though obscured, in our own day in the efforts of Judaism to be both a witness to world community and to realize its destiny as a distinct nation. Now as in the past the tension is connected with the tendency of a universal and radical monotheism to become abstract, a purely individual and spiritual attitude divorced from the concrete life of the people, while henotheism readily presents itself incarnate in total social existence.

The struggle which the Christian sees going on among the Hebrews of history and in modern Judaism is more immediately enacted in his own religious community. He has not been exempted from the temptations of falling into social particularism, however much the captain of his faith overcame the temptation to interpret sonship to God as implying special privilege in relation to a special god. The Christian is not only a Gentile whose sense of the holy and whose reliances on supernatural aid have been reorganized by the radical faith mediated to him by Jesus Christ. He is also the member of a new community, of a people chosen for service in bearing witness to the One beyond all the many, elected to live by, and to mediate to others, confidence in the principle of being itself and loyalty to its cause. In that situation, however, he finds himself and his community tempted constantly to turn faith in being into faith in a special, a social god. He tends to worship a supernatural being who is the collective representation of his own community or who is the principle of its being; to make his center of value that which bestows value on the members of the special society and to define his loyalty as commitment to that society as though it were the ultimate cause. Like the Jew he also can turn the idea of election for service into the idea of elevation to status; he also can define the neighbor as the fellow member of the religious in-group. He also tends to substitute for loyalty to the realm of being, conformity to a social demand; however in his case, in distinction from the Jew, the demand is more likely to be one for right belief (which he may define as Gospel) more than for right action (which he may define as Law). The movement toward the god of the closed society is no less marked in Christianity than it is in Judaism.

Henotheism in Christianity tends to take one of two forms, the church-centered or Christ-centered form. In church-centered faith the community of those who hold common beliefs, practice common rites, and submit to a common rule becomes the immediate object of trust and the cause of loyalty. The church is so relied upon as source of truth that what the church teaches is believed and to be believed because it is the church's teaching; it is trusted as the judge of right and wrong and as the guarantor of salvation from meaninglessness and death. To have faith in God and to believe the church become one and the same thing. To be turned toward God and to be converted to the church become almost identical; the way to God is through the church. So the subtle change occurs from radical monotheism to henotheism. The community that pointed to the faithfulness of the One now points to itself as his representative, but God and church have become so identified that often the word "God" seems to mean the collective representation of the church. God is almost defined as the one who is encountered in the church or the one in whom the church believes. History is reinterpreted so that the story of the mighty deeds of God in creation, judgment, and redemption is replaced by church history or "holy history," an account of special deeds whereby the special community was formed and saved. Rites, instead of being dramatic re-enactments of what God has done, is doing, and will do to men, become divine enactments in a closed society; the deeds of the church or its priests tend to be identified with the deeds of God. The unity of the church, the holiness of the church, and the universality of the church are valued not so much because they reflect the unity, holiness, and universal dominion of God but as ends to be sought for the sake of the church or as virtues to be celebrated because in them the true being of the church comes to appearance. In such ecclesiasticism echoes of monotheism continue to be heard. The God to whom reference is made in every act of worship and in every proclamation of the church's message is still to some extent acknowledged as the principle of being. Yet the confusion is there between that objective principle and its image in the church. The God of the Christian church has become confused with a Christian God, the One beyond all the many with the collective representation of a church that is one community among many.

A second frequent form of the deformation of radical monotheism in Christianity occurs when Jesus Christ is made the absolute center of confidence and loyalty. The significance of Jesus Christ for the Christian church is so great that high expressions about his centrality to faith are the rule rather than the exception in the language of preaching and of worship. Yet it is one thing for Christians to look forward to the day when "every tongue [will] confess that Jesus Christ is Lord, to the glory of God the Father"— to use the words of an ancient liturgical hymn (Phil. 2.11)—and another thing for theology as well as popular piety to substitute the Lordship of Christ for the Lordship of God. At various times in history and in many areas of piety and theology Christianity has been transformed not only into a Christ-cult or a Jesus-cult but into a Christ- or Jesus-faith. The person through whom Christians have received access to God, the one who so reconciled them to the source of being that they are bold to say "Our father who art in heaven," the one who in unique obedience, trust, and loyalty lived, died, and rose again as Son of God, is now invested with such absolute significance that his relation to the One beyond himself is so slurred over that he becomes the center of value and the object of loyalty. The confidence that is expected of Christians is confidence in him; the formulation of the confidence in creed and theology becomes a set of assertions about Jesus Christ; theology is turned into Christology. And with this turn there is also a frequent turn to ecclesiasticism insofar as the community that centers in Jesus Christ is set forth both as the object of his loyalty and of the Christian's loyalty. To be a Christian now means not so much that through the mediation and the pioneering faith of Jesus Christ a man has become wholly human, has been called into membership in the society of universal being, and has accepted the fact that amidst the totality of existence he is not exempt from the human lot; it means rather that he has become a member of a special group, with a special god, a special destiny, and a separate existence. As in the case of church-centeredness such Christ-centered faith, as expressed in cult and theology, remains full of echoes of a radical monotheism. But the tendency toward a henotheism which sets the special principle of the Christian community into opposition with the principle of being is markedly present. In the encounters of Christianity with Judaism and the religions of the East, in the encounters also of the church with other communities in the culture—with states and nations, with academic and intellectual movements—such henotheism is often arrayed against other kinds of social faith; the issue does not always lie between the monotheism of Christianity and the particularisms of non-Christian or non-church movements; sometimes it lies between rival social henotheistic faiths. Sometimes, however, it lies between a Christian henotheism and monotheism more adequately expressed in other apparently nonreligious or non-Christian movements.

Another general observation to be made in this context about the so-called "organized religions" of Judaism and Christianity is that they are not really religions in the narrow sense of that term. Though they are evidently communities in which piety is very important, it is not evident that the activities in which they express their fundamental concerns are of the sort we generally call religious, such as activities of prayer, of reverence for the holy, of expiation. In the case of Judaism this is particularly clear. Judaism centers in the law; on the law of the Lord it meditates day and night. In all its assemblies the presentation of the law has the central position. That law contains statutes concerning worship and prayer, types of sacrifices to be offered, holy days and priestly actions, but it is far more than a law for religious observances. It deals with all aspects of life, and in the history of Judaism those parts of the law that seem most remote from the specifically religious sections have been maintained with even greater fidelity than have the specifically religious statutes. The temple and the sacrifices and the priesthood have disappeared; the synagogue, the Jewish family ethos, the practices of charity, and the proclamation of justice have been maintained. The strains and stresses in contemporary Judaism are manifold; they cannot be reduced to the simple tensions between Judaism as a culture and Judaism as a religion or between Judaism as nationality and Judaism as universal ethics. Nor can they be explained as strains incident to the tendency of religion to permeate the whole of life, unless by religion we mean faith more than piety. It seems inadequate too to describe Judaism as a kind of ethical monotheism if we think of ethics in this connection as something that is added to religious practices directed toward the One. Insofar as the analysis of faith as distinguishable from religion offers us a clue to the situation it appears that what Judaism presents to us —in history and in its contemporary manifestations—is a struggle for the expression of monotheistic confidence and loyalty in the totality of human actions, including religion. The dilemma of Judaism seems to be that its passion for the incarnation of radical faith in the totality of man's life so requires the intensive organization of the life of a people of faith, that this intensive organization leads to a separation and rejection in which the people of faith are tempted to substitute that which makes them one and makes them different—their faith or their culture—for the objective One with whom the faith began. The horns of the dilemma are, on the one hand, intensive incarnation with consequent particularism, or on the other hand, universalism with loss of concreteness. Faith in the One cannot become incarnate short of the realization of a universal human community in which all relations are part of the covenant with the Faithful One; but neither can it become incarnate unless in an intensive way every part of human existence—from religion to eating and drinking—is brought into relation to him. Judaism must insist on the intensive permeation of life by faith in the One. Its creed is always the good news and the commandment:

Hear, O Israel, the Lord our God is one Lord; and you shall love the Lord your God with all your heart, and with all your soul, and with all your might. And these words which I command you this

day shall be upon your heart; and you shall teach them diligently
to your children, and shall talk of them when you sit in your house,
and when you walk by the way, and when you lie down, and when
you rise. And you shall bind them as a sign upon your hand, and
they shall be as frontlets between your eyes. And you shall write
them on the doorposts of your house and on your gates. (Deut.
6.4-9)

But how can such intensity be mated with universality? Or how
can universality achieve such intensity?

In Christianity the dilemma of radical monotheism presents
itself in another way. This community also knows itself to be something besides a religious society that has for its common purpose the
reverence of God, the offering of prayers and supplications to him,
and the practice of a monotheistic piety. It always looks back to
an early ideal of a community that had all things in common;
its Jesus Christ was a healer of diseases, a giver of food, a teacher
of wisdom, a prince of peace as well as a great high priest. It has
sought to express its faith in the establishment and conduct of
Christian states, Christian nations, Christian schools, Christian
families, Christian economics, and Christian philosophies as well as
Christian cults. It is a total ethos, not merely a piety. Yet in distinction from the passion of Judaism for intensive permeation of
life by faith in the One, Christianity has been marked by the passion for universality. It understands that faith in God cannot become incarnate except in a universal community in which all walls
of partition have been broken down. Through Jesus Christ sinners
as well as righteous, Gentiles as well as Jews, and the dead as well
as the living have been given and are to be given access in faith
to the one Father, and by him they are called to loyalty to the one
kingdom. The drive to universality has been present in Christianity
from the beginning; it has been expressed in its expansive and mis-
sionary movements as well as in its efforts to maintain a catholic
church.

But in Christianity radical monotheism meets a dilemma that
is the opposite to the one Judaism encounters. In order to achieve
universality, faith in God and his realm of being now sacrifices
intensity. If every man is to be included in the community of faith,
not all of man can, it seems, be so included. As Judaism has tended
to become a faith culture so Christianity has tended to become a

faith religion and a faith belief. To be sure, the pressure is always present in Christianity toward the total transfiguration of life by faith, as the pressure is present in Judaism toward universalization. But Christianity has tended, far more than Judaism, to define itself as a religion in which all religious practices, all piety, are to be reformed by confidence in God and loyalty to his cause. It is more relevant to describe a Christian as one who goes to a Christian church for worship than to describe a Jew as one who attends a synagogue. The word "church" means for us a place of worship more frequently than it means a people, a community.

It is not possible, of course, to illuminate the whole character of Judaism and of Christianity from the point of view of faith; and the present attempt to deal with Western organized religions as involved in the conflicts of radically monotheistic faith with its rivals, is not an effort to define the essence of Judaism or of Christianity. But one thing seems clear when we attend to the problem of radical confidence and loyalty as it comes to expression in these religions: that is, that the struggle of such faith for victory is no easy thing; that radical faith in the God who is the principle of being itself is given to men as a hope and a goal more than as achievement.

V

Radical Faith in Political Community

FAITH as human confidence in a center and conserver of
value and as human loyalty to a cause seems to manifest itself
almost as directly in politics, science, and other cultural activities as
it does in religion. The struggle between henotheistic and monotheistic faith in the West seems to be nearly as acute in national
as in church life; it may appear in natural science as well as in
theology. Tendencies toward faith-pluralism also appear in the
totality of cultural activities and not in religion alone. So at least it
seems to a theologian who has been led in his critique of religion to
distinguish between faith and other components in the complex
called religion and who has been made aware that Western religion,
whether as piety or as Judaism and Christianity, is continually involved in struggle between the different forms of faith. He can no
longer understand his Western world and its history by considering
the conflicts and accommodations of churches and states, or of
religion and other cultural complexes. Since confidence and loyalty
are not the only components of religion and since Western religion
is not unambiguously monotheistic in its faith, the questions that
arise as he regards other cultural activities are no longer: How
has religion affected them and how have they been affected by
religion? He asks rather: Is faith also expressed in them as it is in
religion? Is the conflict between polytheistic, henotheistic, and
monotheistic faith that is discernible in religion also present in
politics, science, and perhaps in art and economics? He seeks and
gives his answers to these questions with diffidence because whatever competence as critic he has developed has been confined to the

sphere of religion and because he lacks the intimate, internal contact with the other enterprises that valid criticism requires. But he is unable to understand his own special province unless he compares it with others and he has encountered in it features which may be of significance in them. Hence he makes the venture in the expectation of correction and in the hope of some corroboration from those engaged more directly in the reflective analysis of such other cultural activities. With these qualifications in mind, consideration may now be given to radical faith as it is expressed in Western politics and science, confining the discussion, however, in the case of politics, largely to democracy and to the American scene.

1. LOYALTY AND CONFIDENCE IN NATIONAL EXISTENCE

That faith as fidelity to a cause is important in the life of modern nation-states seems to be indicated by the extensive use in politics of the language of loyalty. It is interesting also to note that when we want to find illustrations of the meaning of loyalty which will be intelligible to most modern men we turn most readily to examples taken from the political life. Indeed the word "loyalty" has been so identified with fidelity to political causes that churchmen hesitate to use it in speaking of faith for fear that they be thought to glorify an essentially nationalistic and narrowly patriotic attitude. Yet fidelity, whether practiced in church, home, profession, or nation-state, always has the same general form; it is always a set of mind, a habit of devotion to a cause, and a disciplining of actions in service to a cause. It is distinguishable in each case from fearful obedience to overriding power and from loving attachment to a person or community; its negative form of treason is distinctly different from defiant disobedience and from hatred. When the modern nation-state seeks to elicit loyalty from its citizens it distinguishes itself from the pure power-state that seeks obedience only and from the clan society that counts on uncritical, unquestioning love. Government based on the consent of the governed seems possible only where there is loyalty.

Beyond that, the kind of fidelity on which the modern political community counts and which it seeks to elicit is more than loyalty to the community itself. It has often been pointed out that the modern nation-state is historically peculiar and that one of its distinguishing marks, when compared with ancient kingdoms, is its conception and representation of itself as a community with a mission. It presents itself to its citizens and to those outside as a society pledged to the promotion of a cause transcending itself. It asks for loyalty to itself because it is loyal to such a cause, and it presupposes the direct fidelity of its citizens to the transcendent cause. Many conditions have doubtless contributed to the development of modern nation-states, but among them has been this sense of mission and the conception of themselves as faithful servants of a large cause, significant for other nations and other men. In the case of Spain the national-state represented itself and was believed in as the servant of the true Catholic religion. The United States and France came into being in their modern forms as devoted exponents of democracy and the rights of men. Germany sought its unity as well as power as the exponent of culture. Under the Czars Russia dramatized itself as Holy Russia, a God-bearing people, and its Messianic sense has not been diminished but increased with the substitution of international communism for Orthodoxy. The English nation and the British Empire consciously carried the white man's burden while they enjoyed the perquisites of dominion. The Western nations on the whole have appeared in history as independent powers claiming the right to freedom and self-government as the faithful champions of great human causes. They have resisted aggressions and sought to preserve themselves not simply as powers defying other powers, but as bodies entitled to existence and respect because of their representative character as servants of such ends. In all these nations the loyalty of citizens has therefore had a double direction: on the one hand it has been claimed by the transcendent end, on the other, by the nation itself as representative of the cause. That in this ambivalent, not ambiguous, situation there is much confusion, much hypocrisy, and much self-delusion is all too clear. But to deny the actuality in modern national life of the presence of both kinds of loyalty, to affirm that the only real interest of nations is self-interest and that all reference to great causes is hypocrisy, is to make dogmatic assertions which seem too readily to discount many phenomena in our political existence. It is also to break apart into complete disjunction elements that in human life appear only in indissoluble union—such as self-interest and social interest or conscience and the will-to-power; and it is to ignore the significance of hypocrisy—that tribute which vice pays to virtue and that acknowledgment of a standard which is recognized as binding though not loved. To the theologian a political science that works only with the idea of national self-interest seems very much like the sort of theology which constructs its understanding of man with the use of the idea of sin only, without reference to that good nature which sin presupposes and of which it is the corrupted expression.

Three things, then, seem important when we consider the question whether faith as fidelity is present in political as well as in religious actions and communities of the West. The first is that the nation-states base their existence on the loyalty of their citizens and not only on the latter's fears and desires for benefits; the second, that the nations as communities achieve their unity and justify their existence by pledging their loyalty to transcendent causes; and third, that the loyalty expected of citizens is the double loyalty extended to the nation's cause as well as to nation as cause.

It is not equally clear that in the political communities of the West faith as confidence in a center of value is also present though the general interdependence of trust and loyalty leads one to look for it. Politically we are made most aware of the reference to confidence by the extent to which, as citizens, we are asked to put trust in the nation itself, or in the people, or in democracy. We realize also the extent to which treason is associated with the loss of confidence in the nation, and with the hostility that arises out of a sense of having been betrayed. Insofar as faith is confidence in a center of value which bestows and conserves worth it seems, in political life, as a rule to be the henotheistic or social faith for which the center is the community itself. Yet at least at some points confidence of another sort makes itself manifest, for instance, in connection with some of the doctrines and practices of freedom. Freedom of speech and press and freedom of research can be extended to people in a community only if in the latter as a whole the confidence prevails that truth has power over lie, that it is not the enemy of life or of order or of justice, and that "in the nature of things" truth is mighty. Freedom implies the presence of the assurance that there is a kind of universal government of things, not only of material entities, on which nations as well as individuals can depend. It may, of course, be said that the confidence present in democracies which accord large measures of freedom to their citizens is confidence in the people. But confidence in the people cannot be the basis of freedom if it is believed that the people are always self-interested and can be counted upon only to pursue their private ends. If this were the belief then every care would need to be taken to prevent the individual citizens from defrauding one another; little freedom could be allowed. The kind of confidence in the people that can be the ground for practices of freedom must be assurance of their loyalty to causes that transcend their private interest, including, for instance, devotion to truth. If there is no faithfulness at all among the people to an ideal or cause of truth, or if truth cannot be counted upon in the nature of things to conquer the lie, freedom of speech and of press is a luxury no commonwealth can long afford.

In our political life we seem to be woven together in a web of confidences: confidence in each other; confidence in the nation; the community's confidence in its citizens; their confidence in the community itself and also in transcendent centers of value. And all these confidences are extended to loyalties. We trust only the loyal who are loyal to us and to our common causes. It is easy to see the red and the black networks of suspicion, treason, deception, and lie that run through the common life. But like reticulations of cancerous cells these could not even continue in being were it not for the positive, health-maintaining networks of faith.

2. The Struggle of Social with Monotheistic Faith

It has been difficult to point out the place of faith in political life without becoming involved at once in questions about the forms of such political faith. It almost seems as though faith in its political manifestations is always social and henotheistic. Social faith—confidence in the community itself as source and conserver of value, loyalty to it as the cause—was characteristic, we have noted, of ancient political communities in which magistracy and priesthood, church and state, society and god were identified. It is characteristic also of most modern secular nations which, without benefit of mythology, theology, or metaphysics, so identify themselves with the cause they claim to serve that devotion to the nation and devotion to its cause are blurred into each other; so that reliance on the society is equated with trust in Nature, in Nature's God, or in the determination of destiny by some iron law of history. The U.S.S.R. and Communism are related to each other even more intimately than were Czarist Russia and the Orthodox church; the United States and Democracy are associated in speech and thought more closely than the Bay Colony was with the Reformed religion; the Western nations not only champion but regard themselves as embodying liberal humanism in much the samy way that the Holy Roman Empire identified itself with the Holy Catholic faith. If we analyze the situation with the aid of our concept of faith it is difficult to take seriously the idea that the modern state has become secular and assigned the domain of the sacred wholly to the church. In terms of faith it is often as "religious" as any medieval or ancient community was.

Yet there are manifest differences in the way the doctrines of the political community are held and its principles of action put into effect. In the West, at all events, it is not to be taken for granted that henotheism, in which the political society itself is the center of value and cause of loyalty, is the dominant faith. One thing that gives Western politics its character is the presence in it of a ferment of monotheist conviction and a constant struggle of universal with particularist faith. National faith is forever being qualified by monotheism. It will not do, to be sure, to say that the American nation is intensely God-fearing in a monotheistic sense of God; there is too much evidence to the contrary. Yet God-fearingness, as reverence for the principle of all being and for its domain, is present among us and is in almost daily conflict or tension with our large and small social faiths. We are made aware of the struggle in political life of monotheism with henotheism at two points: in our effort to understand historically some of our great political decisions of the past and in the continuation in present decisions of the policies so laid down. These two—historical understanding and present practice—are closely related. In historical inquiry we find that each of the great decisions has at least a double root; in present decisions to continue inherited policies we discover that we must carry them out in one way or another according to the context of faith in which we make the new resolution.

Freedom of religion in our society may be taken as one case in point. The American nation resolved in the past that the state should make no laws respecting an establishment of religion nor hinder its free exercise; it has followed that resolution with many others until the United States has become the country in which not only many varieties of historic religious organization but many novel prophetisms and enthusiasms flourish. This freedom of religion has a double, if not triple, rootage.[1] On the one hand it derives from the necessity of compromise among manifold religious groups which for the sake of maintaining the national unity tolerate each other and agree with certain political leaders that the issues posed in churches are of less importance than those posed in the state. The idea may take the form of the belief that religion is a private matter or that a man's relation to his god does not affect his value or his effectiveness as a citizen, or that in religion he is concerned with a world wholly distinct from the world of political affairs. In this case religious freedom is the result of the acceptance of the secondary character of all religious loyalties. Religious freedom and religious toleration may then be practiced as they were in the Roman Empire; so long as people can be counted on to make national loyalty supreme, they may be allowed to follow any religion.

But religious freedom has another root in the past and may be presently practiced in another context. It was founded not only on the reflection that national unity is imperiled by the strife of sects so long as each of them can aspire to the exercise of political power; its other source was the acknowledgment that loyalty to God is prior to every civic loyalty; that before man is a member of any political society he is a member of the universal commonwealth in which he is under obligations that take precedence over all duties to the state; and that the state must therefore acknowledge men's rights to perform such duties. Religion, so understood, lies beyond the provenance of the state not because it is a private, inconsequential, or other-worldly matter but because it concerns men's allegiance to a sovereignty and a community more immediate, more inclusive, and more fateful than those of the political commonwealth. Religious freedom understood and practiced in the former

[1]In many instances the triple origin and triple application of national policies is suggested; pluralism takes its place alongside of henotheism and monotheism. In the present discussion the pluralistic aspects of political faith have been left out of consideration for the most part in order that the analysis should not become too complicated and because in my judgment pluralism has usually been subordinated in politics to the social faith. If faith in the realms of economic and poetic or aesthetic activity were analyzed, larger attention would probably need to be paid to pluralism.

context is a grant made by a state exercising sovereign power; understood and practiced in the latter context it is an acknowledgment by the state of the limitation of its sovereignty and of the relative character of the loyalty it is entitled to claim.

Whether today religious freedom is to be practiced in the one context or the other cannot be decided by reference to the mixed sources of past resolutions. The choice has not been made once and for all in the past. It is repeated in daily decisions. The differences in interpretation and practice that result from contemporary decisions made within the context of national loyalty and those made in the context of universal loyalty appear for the most part undramatically, sometimes in judicial decisions and dissenting opinions that do not attract wide attention.[2] Such differences become dramatically apparent only in great crises, as, for instance, in the church-state conflicts of Hitler's Germany. So far we have had no great test in America of the mode of our belief in religious liberty. Insofar as most popular utterances on the subject may be taken as a clue, it seems that Americans are interpreting and practicing religious liberty in general as though its context were simply that of national life. In the thinking of many it is a right bestowed upon citizens by a sovereign nation, not a national acknowledgment of the presence of a sovereign God to whom a loyalty is due that transcends national loyalty. Henotheism and monotheism are in conflict here in the political life, not as church and state are, but within the state itself as in other instances they struggle within the church.

The dual rootage in history of our political dogmas and the alternative contexts in which they may be interpreted in present decision can be illustrated by other democratic principles. The dogma that all power must be limited and the continued practice of

---

[2] The two positions are illustrated, for instance, in Chief Justice Hughes' dissenting and in Justice Sutherland's majority opinion in the Macintosh case. Said Chief Justice Hughes: "In the forum of conscience, duty to a moral power higher than the state has always been maintained. . . . The essence of religion is belief in a relation to God involving duties superior to those arising from any human relation." Justice Sutherland, however, stated that "government must go forward upon the assumption, and safely can proceed upon no other, that unqualified allegiance to the nation and submission and obedience to the laws of the land, as well those made for war as those made for peace, are not inconsistent with the will of God." (*U.S.* v. *Macintosh,* 283 U.S., October Term, 1930.) God and nation are not identified, to be sure, in the latter statement, but the distinction is blurred over in familiar fashion.

balancing power against power, have their origins in the need of finding compromise among rival claimants to authority if national loyalty is to be supreme; but also in the conviction that ultimate power belongs only to God and that in the nature of things, according to the constitution of the universal commonwealth as it were, finite power is actually limited and works destructively if it is not guarded against the constant temptation to make itself infinite, totalitarian, and godlike. The duality appears also in questions about law—whether its source and the context of its interpretation is the social will or the will of God—a structure of right that pervades the realm of being. The idea of the sacredness of covenants has arisen both out of the social regulation of economic practices and out of the conviction that all the world is based on promise and promise-keeping, that God himself is faithful and requires, as he makes possible, a righteousness of faith among men in all their relations.

When we ask the historical question about the origin of our democratic principles, we are likely to raise it in the confused form of an inquiry into the influence of churches or of religious movements on political decisions. So we ask about Puritanism and democracy, or about Calvinism and the right of resistance against tyrants, or about Judaism and the doctrine of the covenant, or about Catholicism and the doctrine of natural law. While some progress can be made in self-understanding by means of these inquiries, confusion also results partly because the churches and the religious movements have themselves never been wholly free from the influence of social faith. Hence when we speak of "theocracy" in New England, we think quite as frequently of the rule of the preachers as of the rule of God, and the conflict of "theocracy" with democracy appears in part as conflict between church sovereignty and popular sovereignty; when we speak of the Catholic teaching about natural law, we think of the church's claim to be the interpreter of that law; and when we inquire into the Calvinist theory of resistance to tyrants we think of revolutions made for the sake of maintaining a particular creed more than of those made in loyalty to the Universal Sovereign and his realm. But despite the confusion between social will and divine will, or between loyalty to a limited community and loyalty to God, the distinction between the two can be made and seen to be significant not only in conflicts between church and state but in intrastate as in intrachurch conflicts as well.

3. The Democratic Dogma of Equality

In order to summarize our reflections and test them further we shall, finally, attend to the democratic belief in human equality as an instance of faith active in political existence and as a focus of the struggle between forms of faith.

The doctrine or, better, dogma that all men are created equal seems to be a faith statement. We do not deal with it as an expression of opinion about the way in which all things and men in particular came into being. Neither do we accept it as a factual statement based on the observation that all men are equal when compared with each other. Reference is made in it to a common center to which all men are related; it is by virtue and in respect of their relation to that creative center that they are equal. A confidence is expressed that all men have worth because they exist as men and are related to the source of existence. Further, the dogma is a pledge, a promise, a commitment. The self-evident truth is not an observer's statement about facts that do not concern him; it is the basis for a claim and a pledge, namely, the claim and pledge that men shall and will respect each other's rights to life, liberty, and the pursuit of happiness. Having been given life by the source of life, their title to life is recognized as equal to the title of any other human being; having been given the liberty of persons by that power which transcends all human enslavers and liberators, their title to liberty is to be acknowledged as equal to every other man's; having been endowed with the urge for their own well-being, that urge in each is entitled to equal consideration with that of every other man. As a pledge the principle of equality is subject to ever new commitment. It must be re-enacted in decision after decision in courts of law, in legislation, in daily administration of common goods, and in national and international political actions. In its original expression the statement seems genuinely monotheistic, but in all new decisions about its application, the question of monotheist faith and its rivals is raised.

How much this is true appears when we consider the nature of the attacks made upon the principle of equality. Some of them are attacks on the mythological form of the assertion rather than on its affirmation about human value and its inherent promise to treat men equally with respect to their rights to life, liberty, and the pursuit of happiness. The self-evident truth, it is maintained, was self-evident only in the intellectual climate of eighteenth-century opinion with its peculiar mythology of Nature, Nature's God and Nature's Laws. Among those who make this objection there are many who maintain that despite the mythological investiture of the principle, it expresses a "truth" which they must accept and practice. Sometimes such critics wish to substitute a humanistic for a theistic understanding of life and a humanistic faith for radical monotheism. Their humanism, however, as noted earlier, is often only a protest against the narrow faith expressed in much religion. Theoretically, the principle is difficult to define since man is so closely related to all other animate beings. Practically, humanism rarely exists in separation from a reverence for life and a reverence for being that point to the presence in it of more than loyalty to mankind. The distinction, however, between mythological expression and faith that this attack on the creedal form of the dogma of human equality calls to our attention is significant. We encounter here in the realm of politics a problem with which we are familiar in religion.

Attacks on the doctrine, however, are often made less on its mythological form than on its faith content, that is, on the confidence and promise expressed in it. One challenge is made by those who point out that the dogma has no empirical basis; experience teaches us, they say, that men are very unequal. The argument ignores the fact that the upholders of the doctrine do not claim it to be empirical and that the belief that only empirical truths can be self-evident or evident is very much a twentieth-century "truth." However that may be, the assertion that in experience men are not equal can mean only that when we relate them to some finite center of value and measure them in their comparative worth for some particular limited cause, they are very unequal. If, for instance, we ask about their relation to the biological human species as the center of value, we cannot affirm that they are equal. Extreme advocates of eugenics note the great disparity among men as representatives of and contributors to the life of the race; so regarded they are not equally entitled to life, liberty, and the pursuit of their happiness. Yet when, in the name of the biological species, such critics challenge the doctrine of equality, they do not do so on the basis of experience only but of experience guided by reliance on biological human life in the species as the center of value and by a devotion to the enhancement of such life. There is nothing in experience itself that requires such a particularist form of faith.

In the argument from experience reason may be taken as the point of departure. If men are primarily related to the life of reason and it is asked to what extent they are representative of reason, the products of reason, its servants and contributors to its rule, then it is empirically true that they are very unequal. In relation to reason they are not equally entitled to life, liberty, and the pursuit of happiness.

Again, if we ask about the value of men considered in their relation to the life of the nation, their inequality will come into view as is most evident when in times of war we use the standard derived from this faith.

In all these cases, and in any others in which some such finite centers of value or supreme values are referred to, we are not dealing with empirical observations arrayed against the faith statement of human equality. We are dealing with reflections, and observations made in the context of faiths that derive the worth of a being from his relation to a finite value-center and that are devoted to the promotion of a particular realm which derives worth from the center. For the most part the argument from experience is the argument from pluralistic faith. In it reference is made now to this and now to that center of value. Men are unequal in their relations to all the limited gods, all the limited centers of value, and in the contributions they make to all the exclusive causes. But, of course, the inequalities determined in one relation do not coincide with those discovered in another. The national traitor may be a great poet; the criminal a superb physical specimen; the genius be half-mad; a highly rational man a poor citizen. Pluralistic faith can organize no commonwealth but only dependent associations in which for a limited time and for limited purposes men may devote some portion of themselves to a partial cause. Therefore it cannot offer to a political society any real alternative to the dogma of human equality. The considerations which it urges can be useful only within the larger framework of a justice based on equality as efforts are made to give men at least equal opportunities to participate in the many values.

Another attack on the doctrine is made by various exponents of aristocracy. Advocates of white or Nordic supremacy reject the doctrine and refuse to use it as a guide to practice. Here also reference may be made to experience though with less justification and with more emotional appeal to the limited loyalty and dependent confidence of people. In this case also a faith is being expressed. It is hard to understand the hold which the theory of white supremacy, for instance, has upon people unless one takes into consideration that all their sense of being important in the world is tied up with their sense of being members of a special race and all their feeling of value is dependent on the sense of being more valuable than others. How much such confidence in one's own worth depends on the depreciation of others seems indicated by the anti-Semitism of Hitler's Germany and the depreciation of the Negro among American deniers of human equality. The doctrine of the supremacy of a special group is a faith, too, in the sense that it expresses loyalty to a cause and a community. The accompaniment of the denigration of other groups is always the call for solidarity in the supposedly superior group.

The dogma of human equality may be both accepted and rejected by nationalists who set it within a context of social faith. Such men understand and value it insofar as it is intelligible in national terms. They can regard the statement of the Declaration of Independence as a declaration of the national will and can accept the kind of justice that is permeated with the idea of equality as a part of the national unwritten constitution. Because the nation in a series of actions has determined and promised to regard its citizens with equal favor, to make no distinction among citizens between rich and poor, religious and irreligious, Protestants and Catholics, Christians and Jews, white and black; therefore they, as loyal to the nation, promise to deal with their fellow citizens as equal when they sit in jury boxes, participate in school-board and draft-board decisions, or otherwise represent the community. In loyalty to nation such men may achieve a high degree of discipline in discounting their personal likes and dislikes and even the approvals and disapprovals of current public opinion while they dispense an even-handed justice to citizens. Here also there is faith—it looks to the nation as the center of value and pledges itself to nation as cause. The logical consequence of such a social faith is not only the recognition of the right of all citizens of the nation to equal treatment but the denial to strangers of such rights. The doctrine of human equality rests on another confidence and loyalty than this.

Hence we may conclude that while the latter doctrine is indeed the expression of a faith all challenges to it are also faith expressions. In theoretical and practical conflicts about the doctrine we are not dealing with the struggles of faith and reason, or faith and experience, but with antagonisms between the reasonings that go on in the contexts of various faiths. The conflict about equality does not lie between religion and politics but between faiths directly expressed in the political life.

Other doctrines and practices of Western political societies might be subjected to analysis also to see whether or not they express faith and whether or not the conflicts of pluralist, henotheist, and monotheist faith are present in their interpretation and use. Historically and in contemporary practice these forms of faith seem involved in the acceptance and application of such principles as the limitation of power, the sacredness of treaties, government by laws not men, acceptance of majority rule, and respect for minority rights. We appear to be carrying on our democratic politics today under the influences of the rival forms of faith, and democracy is variously shaped by them. In henotheism the voice of the people is the voice of god, or god is the people. Government derives not from the consent of the governed but from their will. The word of the people—or of the majority—is the first and last word to be listened to by legislators and judges. Wrong and right are determined by their choice. National interest in this form of faith is the last interest to be considered; loyalty to nation is the supreme loyalty of citizens and governors.

On the other hand the democratic process may be carried on within the context of monotheistic faith. Then no relative power, be it that of the nation or its people as well as that of tyrants, can claim absolute sovereignty or total loyalty. The power that has brought a nation into being has also elected into existence its companion nations; and the rights of such nations to life, liberty, and the pursuit of their well-being are equal in the universal commonwealth of being. Relying on the ultimate source of being and the ultimate power that conserves beings, men will accept the relativity of all their judgments and continue in their striving to make political decisions that express their universal faith. The question of henotheistic or monotheistic democracy is not the question of national egoism or national altruism; it is not a question about our loves but about our faiths, about our ultimate confidence and our ultimate fidelity.

VI

Radical Faith and Western Science

A THEOLOGIAN must approach the question of the place of faith in Western science with a diffidence even greater than he feels when he poses the like question about politics. And that for at least two reasons. For one, all of us nonscientists in Western society, no matter what our special responsibilities, tend to participate more directly in political than in scientific life. Hence we can reflect critically on political principles with some immediacy though we are far from being political specialists. For another, politics seems more akin than science to religion and ethics; for in politics we also engage in that practical reasoning which accompanies our own behavior with its decisions, choices, and commitments or, in current terms, in these spheres we are concerned with values. In science, on the other hand, men engage in the theoretical reasoning that accompanies observation of the behavior of other beings, that is, of objects; they are concerned in this reasoning, we are accustomed to say, with facts rather than values. Nevertheless, in modern culture no one can escape some direct relation to science; though we do not participate in it intensely yet scientific ways of thought have influenced wide circles. Moreover, fact and value or theoretical and practical reasoning cannot be so divorced from each other that political, ethical, and religious men can reason without theorizing, observing, and being concerned with facts; or that scientific men can develop theory without making decisions and choosing values. Hence I venture to approach scientific activity and the scientific community with the question: Is there in them something akin to that trust-loyalty syndrome that is encountered in religion and of which there are recognizable elements in politics? And is the struggle of the various forms of faith also enacted in science?

78

1. Our Faith in Science

As inquirers into faith and its relations it may strike us not, first of all, that scientists are believers but that they are *believed in*. Our twentieth century is an age of confidence in science. In our culture we tend to believe scientists as, we are told, in another age of faith men believed churchmen. To be sure, we call the content of what we now believe knowledge or science, but for the most part it is direct knowledge only for the scientific specialist while for the rest of us it is belief—something taken on trust. We cannot even say that we believe what we do, and what we call factual knowledge, because we know that if we put ourselves through the discipline of scientific inquiry we shall be able to convince ourselves directly of the content of our beliefs and so convert them into knowledge. This also we have been told; and this also we believe on authority and rarely put to the test. Our beliefs about atoms and their nuclei, about electrons, protons, and stranger particles, about fusion and fission, viruses and macromolecules, the galaxies and the speed of light, the curvature of space and gamma-rays, hormones and vitamins, the localization of functions in the brain and the presence of complexes in the subconscious, the functions of the liver and the activities of ductless glands—these seem to excel in variety, complexity, and remoteness from either personal experience or ratiocination all that earlier men believed about angels, demons, miracles, saints, sacraments, relics, hell, and heaven. Perhaps the distance between what scientists assert and what we ordinary men accept as the meaning of their statements is also greater than was the considerable distance between what churchmen said and what people heard and believed.

Why is this so much an age of trust in science? One reason seems to be that the scientists, or the technologists who are associated with them (a distinction which in our naïve beliefulness we often fail to make), have commended themselves to us by the signs they have wrought. Seeing is believing in all common-sense philosophy. Of course we have not seen, with the eye or the mind's eye, what the scientists have seen with the aid of experiment and in theory but we have seen wonderful signs which, we have been told, are the consequences of their understanding. We believe what physicists and engineers tell us about electricity, sound-waves and light-waves, because we have heard radio and seen television. We believe what the professors of nuclear physics say—or what their interpreters say they say—because we have seen not indeed atomic and hydrogen bomb blasts or nuclear-powered engines but pictures of them. Modern, so-called scientific, man is not too different from his forebears in this respect; unless he sees signs and wonders he is reluctant to believe and, as scientists are wont to complain today, he gets the wonder-worker mixed up now as of old with the seer and prophet. If he did not understand that Einstein somehow made the atomic bomb possible he would probably still listen to Edison with greater respect than he accords to Einstein.

Now, also, as of old there is a second ground for believing our authorities. We believe because they make predictions that come true. Once true and false prophets were distinguished from each other on the basis of the accuracy of their predictions; now science and pseudo-science are discriminated on similar grounds. We believe the astronomers because we have seen eclipses at the predicted hour; we believe meteorologists—somewhat—because storms and fair weather have ensued as they foretold; we believe our child psychologists because our children behave as was promised or threatened. We are somewhat skeptical about our economists because their predictions conflict and at critical junctures have misled us and so we may wonder whether their enterprise is truly a science. Prediction and fulfillment, we note, run through our daily experience from the turning of a light switch to a medical prognosis in the doctor's office; and we understand that they run through all scientific work in laboratory and study.

There is, however, a third ground of interpersonal trust. We believe what scientists tell us because they have been faithful to us; they have been loyal to the human community and its members in their administration of the particular domain for which they have responsibility. That domain, we believe, is the understanding of the natural world in which we live and of which we are a part. In administering that domain the scientific community has been on its guard against error and self-deception, and also against the lie. It has not abused the power its esoteric understanding gives it; it has not used the rest of us as instruments for the private purposes of a special class; it has not deceived us, who can easily be deceived about many things that lie beyond our knowledge.

We have come to have our great confidence in science, I think, because we encounter it not as an impersonal activity but as a community of men with a tradition and a discipline of faithfulness. And one aspect of this faithfulness has been its loyalty to the whole human community. This loyalty has been demonstrated in the effort of scientists to keep the commandment of not bearing false witness against any of their neighbors; they have maintained the implicit covenant into which they entered to communicate their knowledge truly in the whole human community. The ethics of science is not ruled only by respect for fact but by respect also for those to whom facts are communicated. The interpersonal faithfulness of the scientific community appears in this, that it is a truth-telling and not only a truth-seeking society of men. The interpersonal loyalty of the scientific community appears at another point. On the whole, despite the esoteric nature of much modern science and the great advantages which such knowledge bestows on its possessors, the layman has confidence that the specialist is keeping his explicit or implicit promise to use his knowledge, with its power, for the benefit of the whole human society and for each individual in it as though humanity and the individual had a value not derived from their relations to a nation or a caste, or some other special value-center. This confidence appears especially, it seems, in the relations of the layman to biological and psychological scientists and to physicians and psychiatrists. If he did not count on their loyalty to him simply as an existent human being participating in the realm of being he could not entrust himself to their ministrations as now he does. He trusts the scientist as loyal to him with an interpersonal loyalty in a universal human realm.

Reflecting on these things the lay beneficiary of science begins to appreciate the dilemmas in which the scientific community has been placed by the rise to supremacy of nationalist loyalty. He notes the uneasiness with which scientists accept the compulsion of secrecy in those phases of research that might give aid to a national enemy. The universal truthfulness of science has not yet been perverted, he believes, by the imposition of such secrecy, though a second step, moving from secrecy to the use of science for the deception of national enemies, would be such a perversion. Science primarily loyal to a nation, or to some other closed community, speaking truth only to the nation, seeking to benefit only the nation or a class—this would be science operating under henotheistic faith as the theologian sees it; it would be science that found value only in what is valuable to the national center and be loyal only to the national community and its members. That a faith or at least morality is tied up with modern science and that this faith may be either more universal or more provincial has been brought home to the layman by what he has heard of Nazi perversions of medicine and Communist pressures on inquiries in genetics. He notes that problems of value and loyalty arise not only where nonscientists make use of scientific findings but where scientists themselves commit themselves to their tasks within a context. This problem of value and loyalty in science itself is not a scientific problem soluble by scientific means. It is, in theological terms, a question of faith.

At another point also the layman becomes aware of a conflict of faiths within science. He notes the possibility that science may find its center within itself and that it may use him, his nation, his friends, and whatever he values, as instrumental goods for the cause of science. His value and the value of all that he values would then be esteemed wholly by reference to knowledge itself or to "truth" as center of value. Whatever value anything has in that scheme would be its value for science, for instance as the illustration of scientific theory, or as the object of scientific observation and experiment. Such partial valuation, made for temporary purposes and quickly overruled by the consideration that the being in question has another value, is not disturbing. The layman can accept his own role or that of other valuable beings as guinea pigs, provided it is provisional and imposed only with consent. He accepts vivisection, which poses the question of a more than humanistic orientation, despite his faith for which animals have more than scientific value, provided it is carried on with some respect for the nonscientific value of the animal. But he suspects that there is a movement in science which operates on the basis of the principle that man and everything else was made for the increase of knowledge, that "truth" is the key-value and the center of values. Here he discerns the presence of a henotheism not unlike the one he finds in a religion that has turned inward and made its own principle of being into a god of faith.

When we suspect that such restricted orientations of value consciousness and loyalty prevail our confidence in science begins to falter. It is not wholly clear to us that the science in which we had conceived confidence is actually pervaded by universal faithfulness. The science which is subject to the skeptical attitude of the larger community is one in which such universal faith is in conflict with partial, closed-society evaluations and loyalties, whether these be the loyalties of nationalism or of scientism.

2. THE FAITHS OF SCIENCE

A second approach to our concerns about the presence in science of faith and of conflict between its forms seems possible to the theologian without presumption. Instead of beginning with his confidence in the scientists he may begin with his valuations of the scientific enterprise. As he reflects on this he becomes aware of the tendency, first of all, to begin with himself as the center of value— a tendency he suspects all men share with him, as his formulation of the law of original sin also leads him to expect. Insofar as this is his orientation whatever is good for him is really good; what is bad for him, in his best judgment, is really bad. He values and disvalues science and the sciences as they tend to serve his needs, to maintain his physical being, to preserve his personal intellectual synthesis of convictions and ideas, and to promote his large or small ego. He is willing to sustain the scientific enterprise so far as it serves these needs. He is not loyal to it; he has interests in it. Knowledge is valued so far as it is useful power in the service of the self-cause.

More frequently, at least in public demonstrations of his faith, this man approaches science as the kind of churchman or citizen for whom the value-center is the closed society of church or state. As a churchman the question about the value of science becomes for him the question about its value in relation to the church and to the principle of the church. If the principle of the church, on which it depends for its existence, is thought to be the creed the question will be: How are scientific beliefs related to the creed? Science and the sciences will be valued accordingly. If it can be shown or believed, as many have argued, that the basic condition for the rise of modern science was the medieval creed of the churches, then churchly henotheism values science if not as the church's child at least as its first cousin. If science is out of harmony with the creed it may still be regarded as an errant child that will eventually mend its ways. When its theories can be used for the support of the creed and the church it may be valued not as sinner but as saint.

When the principle of the church is conceived more ethically than creedally, more as a "spirit" informing the will than as a "spirit" presiding in the mind of the community, then sources of science in the humanitarian ethos of Christianity may be brought into view and it will be valued as a creation of neighbor-love. It will be appreciated and depreciated also in its present activities in accordance with its relation to love as the cause to be served. Then so-called applied science will be highly regarded insofar as it contributes to human welfare. The value of pure science will be questionable.

A closed-society Biblicist, who does not look beyond the Bible, in the direction toward which the Bible points, but centers on the Bible itself as the principle of the church or of Christianity, will value science by its relation to that book. He may prize archaeology of a certain sort as the chief of the sciences. In the conflicts of religion and science the presence of such henotheistic faiths within the church has played a significant role, though it would be wrong to locate the source of all the conflicts there or to think that in religion only we are subject to the temptations of henotheism.

We make a similar faith evaluation of science today as members of national society. Historically, it seems that the alliances and conflicts between religion and science have been replaced by the alliances and conflicts between nation and science. But the latter also takes place under the aegis of a closed society. The utility of science in developing weapons and methods of national defense, in increasing the nation's economic wealth, power, and glory makes it highly valuable. Some reverence for it as the creation of the national genius may also occasionally be present, yet fundamentally it is appreciated as the instrument of national loyalty more than as the creation of the national genius. Hence also arises the use of a standard of evaluation, apparently most distasteful to many scientists, which prizes more highly the technical achievements science makes possible than science itself, and socially useful inquiries more than insights that have no foreseeable significance for national survival, power, and glory.

The external observer cannot but overhear the complaints of the scientific community against these evaluations of its worth and against the kinds of support or antagonism it must endure as a result of these various loyalties. The question which arises for an observer who has learned, not without aid from science, to be critical of his own narrowly based evaluations is whether the judgments science makes of other enterprises and the support it renders them is sometimes similarly founded on a closed-society orientation of its own; whether in the alliances and conflicts of political, religious, humanitarian, and scientific communities the last of these is indeed always on the side of the universal against the particularism present in the others. It seems to such an observer that at times in the scientific community, as in the religious, a creed may come to be regarded as the absolute principle on which science itself is thought to depend for its being and by reference to which all other human beliefs, and indeed the significance of all beings or phenomena, are judged. The mechanistic creed, for instance, seems to have played such a role in long periods in past centuries and for large sections of the scientific community. As in the case of the church the question about such a creed is not whether it is valuable but whether it is the ultimate standard by which all other beliefs are judged; whether it itself is made the object of commitment and devotion. Or, the closed-society faith of science can concentrate on scientific method as the church can concentrate on its own ethos. It does not seem entirely a figure of speech to say that sometimes for some of the devotees of science, if not for scientists themselves, the scientific method has become a god. It determines, if not all value, then at least all truth; what it reveals is held to be indubitably true, what is untrue for it is false. Sometimes the more enthusiastic believers seem to look to it also for the determination of the good and beautiful. Indeed a churchman would hardly dare to raise any questions about a phrase he has learned from his society to approach with a sense of reverence and feelings of the holy had he not heard from many a scientist statements like President Conant's: "It would be my thesis that those historians of science, and I might add philosophers as well, who emphasize that there is no such thing as the scientific method are doing a public service."[1] I know some men for whom such a statement has the ring of blasphemy. For the observer the question is not whether there is a scientific method; the question is whether science can so concentrate on it that this one discipline immanent in men, this one "spirit" among the many "spirits" in our world, becomes for it an absolute, a center of devotion, and an ultimate cause.

Again, the scientific community in its alliances and conflicts with other communities gives evidence of the presence of a closed-society faith when it exalts truth as the central value and the final

[1] James B. Conant, Modern Science and Modern Man, 1952, p. 19.

end to be pursued not simply by the scientific community or by man in his role of scientist, but by all men and always. Then it seems to rely on truth to bring forth justice, welfare, integrity, peace, and all other goods. Then man exists for the sake of truth and truth is not a part of a complex system of values in subjects and objects in a complex world of being. True knowledge then is no longer the limited cause which with true justice, true beauty, and true religion receives the devoted service of one special group among many in a community that has a center and a cause beyond all these vocational ends; it becomes the exclusive cause to which all others are thought to be secondary and inferior. In practice such exclusiveness may rarely be found; but it is not infrequently expressed in the confused words which equate truth with ultimate value and make science the sole devotee of truth.

A theologian would not be so aware of the prevalence in science of the kind of closed-society faith he has encountered in religion did not scientists themselves in their constant self-criticism call these things to his attention. Without such self-criticism in the scientific community he might be the more tempted to fall back on his own tendencies toward henotheistic thinking and would tend to oppose the faith of his religious in-group to that of a scientific out-group. But as he attends to the self-questionings of scientists he senses that the issues present in their enterprise have a similarity to those with which he is concerned in religion. He thinks that he discerns alongside of the tendencies toward closed-society orientation in science a fundamental movement that is like the radical monotheism he encounters in religion and of which he sees the presence in political issues.

Something like the radical faith in the principle of being as center of value and in the realm of being as cause, seems to the theologian to be present first of all in a negative form in the established habit of scientific skepticism toward all claims to absolute significance on the part of any finite being and of the absolute truth of any theory of being. In the endeavor of science to rid itself of all anthropomorphism and anthropocentrism, of all tendencies to regard man as the measure of all things, whether of their nature or their value, he notes the presence of movement like that of radical faith in religion. Conflicts of science with religion he sees have occurred at least as often between anthropocentric religion and a science that challenged such concentration on man as between science that started with human reason as the measure of all things and a religion that regarded this beginning as idolatrous. Scientific skepticism has dethroned also the efforts to define all things and processes in terms of number or after the model of the machine. In this negative movement of scientific skepticism something is present which is like that *via negativa* in the religion which denies the name of God to any limited form or power, not because it doubts the reality of the One beyond the many but because it believes in him.

More positively radical faith in that One seems present to the theological point of view in the confidence with which pure science seems to approach anything and everything in the world as potentially meaningful. It does not assert explicitly nor does it imply, as universal religion and ethics do, that whatever is, is good. But in its domain it appears to move with the confidence that whatever is, is worthy of attention. Like pure religion pure science seems to care for "widows and orphans"—for bereaved and abandoned facts, for processes and experiences that have lost meaning because they did not fit into an accepted framework of interpretation. Whatever is, in the world of being and becoming, is worthy of inquiry not because of its intrinsic worth nor yet because it is part of some familiar pattern of meanings, but because it *is*, because in its existence it participates in being and is related to the universal and the unitary. How it is so related pure science does not yet know; but it pursues knowledge with apparently unshakable confidence that relation there is and that something universal appears in each particular. Not all events or things are equally revelatory of universal meanings to be sure, but all are participant in them. In their words scientists may express great skepticism about the unity of the world of being, but the external observer continues to marvel at the confidence with which in patience and despite many defeats the quest for universally valid knowledge of the particular is carried on. Attention seems to be given to the most unlikely phenomena in the assurance that the relatedness of the apparently unrelated will appear, though at its appearance a transvaluation of all previous scientific values may be necessary.

There is a loyalty also in pure science that is like the fidelity associated in universal religion with radical faith in being. Science always involves commitment; the scientist devoting himself to his work must accept the arduous discipline of service to a cause. Usually that cause is simply called "knowledge" or "truth" to distinguish it from the causes served in religion, art, or politics. But when this is done a fundamental problem is obscured and the issues between science and religion or politics are confused. The cause of the pure scientist does not seem simply to be knowledge or truth but universal knowledge, universal truth. He carries on his work with "universal intent,"[2] as one who seeks a truth that is true of universal relations and true for all subjects in the universe. This cause is distinguished not only from the causes of religion, art, and politics but from commitments to knowledge with a particularistic intent, or from devotion to truth that might be true for some subjects only. The conflict of science with religion has been conflict less with the religious element in religion—with reverence for the holy, for instance—than with the dogmatic "truth-systems" of closed-society faith; its conflicts with politics have been with the dogmatic "truth-systems" of closed political societies as well as with their power interests. Science which makes universal truth its cause takes its place alongside universal religious faith and the politics that is guided by universal loyalty, not without tension to be sure, but with some community of spirit.

It would be possible, I believe, for someone more adequately equipped to carry this analysis of the forms of human faith into other spheres of activity than those of religion, politics, and science. The humanities and especially literature offer a rich field of inquiry not only into the problem of how faith is expressed in life but into the other problems of the forms of faith that are so expressed, and of their conflict. Such an inquiry would raise more directly than the present attempt has done the question of humanism. Is not the alternative to all pluralistic and henotheistic, to all individualistic and closed-society forms of faith, a humanistic confidence and loyalty? Speaking in Durkheim's terms, does not the issue lie between those whose god is the collective representation of a special group and those who trust in and are loyal to the collective representation of mankind as a whole?

There is a historical answer to that question. Modern humanism to a large extent is, as previously pointed out, a protest against henotheistic faith, especially in the realm of religion. It is a protest, in the name of a larger trust and more inclusive loyalty, against those

---

[2] The phrase is Michael Polanyi. Cf. his *Personal Knowledge—Towards a Post-Critical Philosophy*, 1958; especially Chap. 10.

forms of faith that put their confidence in some exclusive principle. Insofar as it is a protest against theism it is often a protest against henotheism disguised as monotheism. Historically, however, humanism is the affirmation of the value of all men and as the acceptance of the vow of loyalty to the whole human community has flourished only within the framework of radical monotheism. Symbolically speaking the revelation of the Son of man has occurred only within the context of the revelation of the principle of being as God.

Genuinely radical monotheism has included all that humanism includes and something more. It has affirmed not only all mankind but all being. It has involved men not only in battle against the wrongs that afflict men but set them into conflict with what is destructive and anarchic in all accessible realms of being. Its religion has found holiness in man, but also in all nature and in what is beyond nature. It has believed in the salvation of men from evil, but also in the liberation of the whole groaning and travailing creation. Its science has sought to understand men, yet for it the proper study of mankind has been not only man but the infinitely great and the infinitely small in the whole realm of being. Its art has reinterpreted man to himself but has also re-created for man and reinterpreted to him natural beings and eternal forms that have become for him objects of wonder and surprise.

Radical monotheism as the gift of confidence in the principle of being itself, as the affirmation of the real, as loyalty—betrayed and reconstructed many times—to the universe of being, can have no quarrel with humanism and naturalism insofar as these are protests against the religions and ethics of closed societies, centering in little gods—or in little ideas of God. But insofar as faith is given to men in the principle of being itself, or insofar as they are reconciled to the Determiner of Destiny as the fountain of good and only of good, naturalism and humanism assume the form of exclusive systems of closed societies. A radically monotheistic faith says to them as to all the other claimants to "the truth, the whole truth and nothing but the truth," to all the "circumnavigators of being" as Santayana calls them: "I do not believe you. God is great."[3]

---

[3] See Spinoza, *Ethics*, Everyman's edition, 1910, Introduction by George Santayana, p. xxii.

Supplementary Essays

I

Theology in the University *

THE question about the place of theology in the hierarchy or the anarchy or the republic of the human sciences, arts, and critiques has, of course, always been of great interest to theologians. They have had a personal stake in the acceptance by the intellectual community of philosophies of education and of the organization of studies. For these have so often either enthroned them in the realm of learning or completely banished them to the outer darkness of obscurantism and superstition. Today the question, however, has become a matter of concern to many nontheologians as they reflect on the complex character of our civilization, on the religious elements in our political, literary, and scientific traditions and, more specifically, on the nature and function of those centers of civilization, the universities.

There are some, theologians and nontheologians, who see the universities involved in a great crisis; they find only anarchy prevailing in what was once, they believe, a beautifully harmonious universe of learning. They tend to look with nostalgia toward a mythical golden age when stable order prevailed in the intellectual centers of society. Then, they think, academic lions and lambs lived in peace under the benign government of Queen Theology; and all the faculties—of schools as well as of men—worked together for good. In that beautifully ordered hierarchy of learning and instruction first things always came first; the intellectual virtues were properly exalted above moral or civil excellence; and in the cultivation of those virtues ultimate values—the grand old trinity of the beautiful, the good, and the true—were given rightful precedence over mere facts, over the empirical, the natural, and the historical as proper objects of contemplation. To those who cherish this remembrance of a golden age the great desideratum is the re-estab-

* Essay formerly entitled "Theology—Not Queen but Servant" from *The Journal of Religion*, January 1955.

lishment of theological sovereignty.

Something very important is often forgotten by the believers of this myth. In the spotted reality of the medieval world it was not theology that governed the universities; it was rather the highly visible church. So also it was not metaphysics but the city-state that dominated the thought of Greece and it is not natural science but the nation-state and economic utilitarianism that tend to control intellectual life today. It is also forgotten that theology no less than other human inquiries was in servitude then; and that when the great emancipation took place theology no less than humanistic studies and natural science participated in the revolt. It did not abdicate a rule it never held; it pointed rather to a sovereignty that no human institution—whether a church or a state or a science— could usurp without inviting catastrophe.

The modern university developed amid the complex interactions of Renaissance, Reformation, and nationalism; of religious awakenings, of the rise of natural science, modern technology, and popular government. In that confused history theology sometimes played only a minor role; sometimes it became the servant of other human sovereigns—of states using churches and schools for the sake of achieving national conformity, or of popular opinion trying to speak with the voice of God. Servant to these, it sometimes functioned for them as taskmaster and censor of other studies. But whenever it returned to its proper loyalty and achieved its own freedom to serve only its Lord, it also contributed to the liberation of other sciences and institutions from servitude to finite dominion. The other side of the picture is this: whenever some pretender to absolute sovereignty arose in the past, it was usually theology that first of all he sought to buy or cudgel into servitude and, failing that, to eradicate. Never the queen, theology has always had to choose whom it would serve and in what service to find its freedom.

Today it sometimes seems as if in the various human communities—the intellectual as well as the political and religious—no choice were left to us save the one between a complete pluralism and an absolute, though artificial, monism. On the one hand we can continue, it appears, in the direction of what, theologically regarded, is a proliferating polytheism; on the other hand we are asked to submit for the sake of order and peace to some overlordship, whether this be exercised in the name of a nation or cause whose security is valued beyond all other goods, or of a movement that promises to deliver man from evil by five-year stages. Polytheism is as real in reputedly irreligious modern society as ever it was, though now the gods go by the name of values or of powers. With religious zeal we serve truth for truth's sake only, health for health's sake, life for life's sake, man for man's sake, nation for nation's sake. These many objects of devotion are further pluralized into many kinds of truth, presented in many mutually untranslatable languages; into many individual men, many nations, and many lives irreverent toward each other. The greater the fragmentation the greater is the peril—and the attractiveness—of some monistic organization of study and devotion. Ought we not then to organize this anarchic polytheism into a pantheon governed by the most attractive value or the most dynamic power of the moment?

The radically monotheistic theology that played a part in earlier reformations of churches, nations, and universities points, I believe, to another alternative. To be sure, as a theology of protest against the assumption of sovereignty by any finite power or against the presumption of any human voice to speak the ultimate word it seems to invite pluralism and fragmentation in schools, churches, and nations. But the protest is only the negative side of the positive conviction which such theology seeks to demonstrate. This is the conviction that there is an ultimate word, a word of God; that there is a universal Sovereignty, or better, that the universal power, whence come life and death, is good; it is the conviction that man when he is right in any way—right in inquiry, right in thought, right in conduct, right in belief—is right by faith, right by virtue of his reliance upon and his loyalty to the last word and the universal Sovereign. Such theology does not undertake to be the science of God for it knows that the Transcendent Universal is known or acknowledged only in acts of universal loyalty and in transcending confidence, precedent to all inquiry and action. Loyalty and confidence of that sort, it knows, are not demonstrated more in so-called religious acts of mind or body than in so-called secular activities. Hence it calls attention to the way in which every individual, group, and institution is directly related to the Transcendent—whether positively in trust and loyalty or negatively in distrust and disloyalty.

The part that these convictions have played in the political field in the development of what we call democracy has again become the subject of considerable discussion. What does it mean to a state that it is "under God"; without absolute sovereignty; directly responsible to the Transcendent; one institution among many with similar responsibilities to the same One; having citizens who are first of all citizens of another, prior, and universal Commonwealth? The alternative to pluralistic democracy in which every man is a king or every minority or majority group the court of last resort is not a dictatorship of an individual or a class or of the common will, but a democracy in which loyalty to the universal Commonwealth and its Constitution is maintained though no single human power or institution—including the church or the people—can represent that Great Republic or do anything except point to it and try to be loyal to it.

Perhaps the theological idea of a university is as little realized anywhere in the world today as is the radically monotheistic idea of democracy. But as the latter is an ingredient in the life of many nations so the former seems to be hiddenly present in the activities of many intellectual societies. At least it seems so to the theologian. He finds many colleagues in the university who will not or cannot speak his language in whom the essential elements of what he calls "life in faith" are present. They practice, without confessing, a universal loyalty; they count upon the victory of universal truth and justice; they exercise a constant repentance, a *metanoia*, in self-examination and the search for disinterestedness; their scientific humility seems to have a religious quality. But whatever be the present situation it seems worthwhile that we should examine some of the main features of the idea of such a university.

It is in the first place a university which takes its place alongside church and state and other communities or institutions without subordination to any one of these. It is as directly responsible to the Transcendent in the performance of its particular duties of study and teaching as they are in their administration of the laws or in their preaching and worship. It is under obligation to try to understand what is true for all men everywhere in the universal community and to communicate the truths it understands without bearing false witness against any neighbors, whatever be their loyalties or privileges. Located in a nation, it is not of the nation but of the universe; though it is part of a culture, it cannot but try to transcend the outlook of that culture.

Further, this theological idea of a university is the thought of a community of learning which is undergirded by the confidence that the nature of things is such that bias, deceit, and falsehood, issuing from individual and social self-interestedness, cannot in any long run—in the final judgment, so to speak—triumph over honesty and rigorous self-discipline in study and communication.

Again, it is the idea of a university in which the intellectual virtues neither assume priority over the moral goods of character nor assert their independence, but where the intellect is directed toward the universal in an intellectual love of all truth in God, an intellectual confidence in the unity of all truths in him, an intellectual hope of salvation from error and falsehood as well as from ignorance. As universities, churches, and states exist alongside each other in mutual service and mutual limitation—interacting communities in one great commonwealth—so the intellectual activities are carried on in constant interaction with civil and moral activities and with the religious exercise of proclamation, prayer, and confession. There have been times, indeed, when theology has undertaken to substitute for the old aristocratic idea of the supremacy of the intellectual virtues a romantic exaltation of the life of feeling or a nominalist, pragmatic assertion of the priority of will. But under the discipline of its own fundamental convictions it has again rejected these new hierarchies, acknowledging that the problem is not whether heart or mind or strength should be supreme but whether each should be directed toward the Universal and Transcendent or perverted toward the particular and exclusive. And this seems to be in accord with experience, for the battles of the intellect for freedom are directed less against sentimentalism and willfulness than against pettiness of mind and intellectual dogmatism, as the problem of the will is not so much the problem of maintaining itself against reason as of learning to say, "Not my will be done, but Thine." It is a poor theology that makes human reason the image and representative of God, but the theology that puts feeling, albeit a religious feeling, or moral will above reason in the service and similitude of God is no less idolatrous.

In a university in which the radically monotheistic idea comes to expression, the various departments, schools, and methods are related to each other in mutual service, including the service of mutual limitation and creative conflict. The theology of radical monotheism knows that the second commandment is implicit in and equal to the first. If the first requirement on every man in every action is loyalty to the Universal and Transcendent its corollary is loyalty to all other beings emanating from and proceeding toward that Begin-

ning and End of all. A kind of equalitarianism must prevail therefore in the universal society, not only as among individual men,
communities, and cultures but among the orders of being. Matter
and spirit, mind and body, nature and supernature proceed from
the one source and are bound together in one community in which
there is no high or low, no hierarchically ordered chain of being,
but in which each kind of being is entitled to reverence, understanding, and service, while it in turn is servant to the rest. And as
all beings are bound together in mutual dependence so the students
of their natures and their relations are necessarily united in interdependent service.

There is another element in the equalitarianism of such a university. In it the common recognition is present that pretension to
deity is universal among men; that in one way or another we all
try to play God. Preachers and priests and theologians want to be
theocrats, but so in their own way do the guardians of other traditions and the seekers after another knowledge. Economic interpretations of history and psychological interpretations of the self and
naturalistic explanations of the way all things came into existence
take their place alongside ecclesiastical orthodoxies. Where this is
known and acknowledged, where it is understood and confessed—
with irony and humor—that all of us are involved in this preten-
tiousness, there limitation and criticism by each other, even occasional humiliation, is not resented but reluctantly welcomed as a
kind of mutual service. Creative conflict prevents such a university
from being too beautifully ordered to be alive, since all real life
involves tension and even conflict.

In a university ultimately controlled by such a faith, theology can
by no means be queen. Insofar as it is theology based on confidence in God and on loyalty to the Universal Community, radically
monotheistic rather than polytheistic in character, it can ask only
for a place of service. It enters into the company of the sciences
and studies not to be ministered to but to minister. To be sure, it
must scorn the role of sycophant, for it has its own responsibility
and freedom under God. It looks with distaste on the kinds of
activities that call themselves theology but which, instead of being
concerned with man's relation to God, are efforts at the self-
justification of human religion whether in the presence of the community of natural science or of a society intent on the achievement
of national security or of individual peace of mind. It knows itself

to be first of all servant of God. It does not presume to believe that because it is concerned with the knowledge of God it is therefore pre-eminently his servant. On the contrary, it realizes that its temptations to try to be more than servant are perhaps greater than those of other studies. But in the service of God it is also the servant of its fellow servants. It is servant of the church, seeking to serve the faith that the church, when it is really church, tries to express in word and deed. Theology is not automatically church any more than grammar is necessarily communication or logic wisdom. Its function is service to the church, by means of the criticism of actual religion and through the effort to help the church understand what it believes. The theology which is servant to the church under God is also servant of the university and of political society, since it is not only the church that is in the kingdom of God and since faith exists and does its work not only in the church. Within the university theology does not undertake to render service in the freedom of the uncommitted, but this is not a loss of freedom since the wholly uncommitted are free only to serve themselves. It cannot seek truth for its own sake, but only for the sake of the divine glory—truth as reflection of the nature of being itself. Insofar as it does that, seeking truth not for the sake of the church's glory or in order to glorify anything at all except the Transcendent Source and End of all things, its work in the university will not be less free than that of other inquiries. It ought to be the freest of all. As fellow servant of truth in this sense theology takes its place in the university alongside other inquiries, never separated from them, never dependent upon them, never isolating itself with them from the totality of the common life which is the universe.

Sometimes, indeed, our faith grows very dim. Is not this world a pluriverse in which a scattered human race wanders aimlessly, fights fruitlessly, moves toward nothing? But then the gift of faith returns; confidence is resurrected; or as Chesterton puts it, the flag of the world is unfurled. In such moments theology is reborn; then we re-establish and reorganize our universities; we call our scattered churches together and summon our states to abandon their fears and to maintain the unity of mankind. In such hours theology takes pride in her handmaiden's role.

II

The Center of Value*

WHATEVER may be the general reflections of value theorists on the meaning and nature of "good," when they deal with more concrete ethical problems they usually employ a relational theory of value which defines good by reference to a being for which other beings are good. Insofar as Plato's *Republic* is concerned with the good-for-man, man's psychical structure is the starting point for the determination of what is good. Nikolai Hartmann, having defined value abstractly as essence, as that which ought-to-be without dependence on the existent, turns in his ethics to the question of the good-for-man, confining his analysis of values to the virtues—the kinds of excellence appropriate to man—and insisting that the freedom of man must always be considered so that his question really is, "What is good for free man?" G. E. Moore, after attempting to indicate the meaning of value in abstraction from every relation, assumes the standpoint of conscious, social man as soon as he undertakes to answer the question, "What things, then, are good?" He answers, "By far the most valuable things, which we can know or can imagine, are certain states of consciousness, which may be roughly described as the pleasures of human intercourse and the enjoyment of beautiful objects." It is not possible for Moore to read out of the picture the being for whom these things are good, however much he may speak of the intrinsically good. He employs a relational theory of value though he asserts that "personal affection and the appreciation of what is beautiful in Art or Nature, are good in themselves." He has posited a being with consciousness and sociality as that for which these things are good, not as desired but as desirable, as necessarily complementary to its existence.

As intuitionists and rationalists move from their objective theories

* From *Moral Principles of Action*, edited by Ruth Nanda Anshen (Harper & Brothers, 1952).

of value to relational views when they turn to ethics, so the empiricists also seem to abandon their subjectivist views when they deal with concrete questions. Hume has greater awareness of what he is doing than is the case with many of his followers, for though he seems to regard value as a function of feeling, yet he considers that judgments about moral values have a rational character, not only in the sense that they abstract from personal feelings and consider virtues and vices in relation to social feeling expressed in approval or disapproval, but in the more objective sense that they are directed toward what is useful to society. His discussions, to be sure, are so confined to the consideration of "moral" values, i.e., to virtues and vices, that the larger pattern of his relational theory does not come to complete expression. Yet it is clear that he not only employs but argues for the validity of an ethical theory which makes society its starting point and inquires into the comparative goodness for society of self-love, benevolence, fidelity, and so forth, in its citizens. Though he mates agreeableness with usefulness to society the latter relation is always in his view, and in his context it is not a narrow means-end idea. The shift from subjectivism to relational theory is accomplished with apparent unawareness of the change by Bentham as he moves from explicit hedonism with its desire theory of the good to utilitarianism with its question about what is good for society as represented by the greatest number of its individual members.

Similar movements of thought from subjective relativism to relationism may be noted in Westermarck, Schlick, and A. J. Ayer. For Westermarck as for Hume the assertion that good depends on emotion soon makes place for the idea of *disinterested* moral emotion which observes the relation of a moral quality to the emotions of a society, and this understanding is then supplemented by a theory of usefulness. For it is assumed that the disinterested moral emotion is itself good for social life, that specific institutions or customs were originally approved because of their utility, and that "correct utilitarian considerations" can and should be employed in criticizing mores which are maintained by feelings only. In this case as in Hume's, *usefulness* means far more than simple means-to-an-end. Schlick thinks that "the question whether something is desirable for its own sake is no question at all, but mere empty words. On the other hand, the question of what actually is desired for its own sake is of course quite sensible, and ethics is actually concerned only with answering this question." Again, " 'value' is nothing but a name for the dormant pleasure possibilities of the valuable object." Yet when he turns to the question, "What then is good?" he posits the social human being with capacity for happiness and designates kindness as the good which corresponds to that capacity, not because it pleases all men but because it is in conformity with human nature. The value of kindness is not relative to actual feelings of pleasure but stands in such relation to the capacity for happiness that it is possible to make the judgment that kindness is good for man with his social impulses and his capacity for happiness. Though Ayer dismisses the term "value" or "good" as nothing but the expression of an emotion, he employs relational value theory in his contention that the scientific method is of great importance to man. Evidently he does not regard this statement as an emotional ejaculation but argues that science is good for man because it is the useful instrument by means of which he is enabled to survive and to meet his needs, even the simplest.

The relational value theory which is implicit in the ethical reflections of such objective or subjective value theorists is objective in the sense that value relations are understood to be independent of the feelings of an observer but not in the sense that value is itself an objective kind of reality. The statement that "justice is good" or that "justice ought to be" may be regarded by some as an emotional outburst equivalent to the statement, "I like justice." By others it may be defended as a verbal formulation of a direct intuition of objective value, but it is difficult to see what difference there is between such subjectivism and such objectivism so far as the consequences of the opposing positions are concerned. The indefinable cannot be used in communication or analysis. Yet the statement that justice is good for a society with many parts, in the sense that a just-right relationship between such parts must be sought in order that the society may live and realize its potentialities, is an objective statement which an observer can make quite apart from his intuitions or his desires. Furthermore, the meaning of the term "justice" in this situation is subject to specific analysis on the basis of prior inquiry into the constitution of the society. Relational value theory agrees with objectivism on this further point, that what is good-for-man, or for society or for any other being which represents the starting point of inquiry, is not determined by the desire of that being. Whether food or poison is good for animal existence has little to do with the desires in such existence; whether error or truth is good for mind has little connection with the desire of an intellectual being for one or the other. What is fitting, useful, and complementary to an existence can be determined only if disinteredness, or abstraction from desire, is practiced and the nature and tendency of the being in question are studied. Yet relational value theory does not pretend that value has existence in itself, that independence from desire is equivalent to independence from the being for which the valuable has worth. It agrees with the subjective value theory insofar as the latter regards value as relative to being, disagreeing, however, with the relativism which makes the good relative to desire rather than to need, or which makes it relative to man as absolute center of value.

In view of the manner in which relational value-thinking has been intertwined with the *motifs* of objectivism and subjectivism it is desirable that its main points should be set forth as clearly as possible without reference to these complicating strains of thought. Its fundamental observation is this: that value is present wherever one existent being with capacities and potentialities confronts another existence that limits or completes or complements it. Thus, first of all, value is present objectively for an observer in the fittingness or unfittingness of being to being. In the one case it is present as positive, in the other case as negative value; it is present as good or as evil. Whether the starting point be a biological existence in the presence of a fitting or an unfitting environment, or a society in the presence of another society as friend or enemy, or mind confronting patterns, ideas, chaos, or brute power in the data given to it—in every case there is good or evil in this situation. Good is a term which not only can be but which—at least in the form of one of its equivalents—must be applied to that which meets the needs, which fits the capacity, which corresponds to the potentialities of an existent being. It is, in this sense, that which is "useful." Evil, on the other hand, is that which thwarts, destroys, or starves a being in its activities.

Yet the situation in which good and evil occur is, it is apparent, not only one of reciprocity among existent beings. It is also one in which such existences are in a state of becoming, in which they are not yet what they "ought" to be—not in any legal sense of the word "ought" but in the sense that they have not yet achieved their own internal possibilities of becoming good for others, or of supplying to others in the community of being what they "owe" them. Medicine is good for the sick in view of their movement toward health, which is good for the self in relation to other selves and other beings in general; education is good for the child in its movement toward the realization of its capacities for activities beneficial to human society, other selves, and other beings in general; science is good for the intellectual life in its development and in its service to the needs of being.

In this situation of being, in process of becoming itself (always as social self) and among others becoming themselves (also as social), value appears in many relations of which two may be particularly distinguished. On the one hand, that is good for a being which, separate from itself, assists it in its realization of its potentialities. On the other hand, the state of realization (the excellent or virtuous state) is good. This latter good is also a "good-for-ness," not primarily as a good for the becoming self but as a good for other beings in its whole community, and then secondarily, in the endless interactions of self and others, a good-for-the-self. The former of these is often called the instrumental good, the latter the intrinsic or end good; but these designations are misleading. For existent being does not seek the complementary good necessarily for the sake of achieving its own state of perfection; it may well seek and serve the complementary good as a kind of end and thereby grow toward its internal good, the realization of its essence, without direct concern for the latter. The mind grows toward the realization of its possibilities by seeking truths about nature and history, but these truths are its ends and its growth may come as by-product. It is not evident that in seeking food the animal uses as instrumental the good which is the object of its direct quest; this is its end-good in the situation while life, health, and physical growth are consequents. On the other hand physical, moral, intellectual, and spiritual excellence is less an end value for the self than a good for other beings. Relational value theory cannot be utilitarian in the sense that it posits a being with its own survival or self-realization in view as its end, a being which thereupon uses as means to the end the complementary goods of environing beings. It must do justice to the fact that value is not dependent on a conscious finalism for which some goods may be designated as intrinsic goods, others as instrumental. There are good states of the self and there are goods-for-the-self which are not self-states. Self-states are goods first of all for other selves, or other beings, and only by indirection goods-for-self. Yet value exists in the reciprocal relations which beings realizing potentiality have to other beings. In this situation every good is an end and every good a means.[1]

The Aristotelian form of relational value theory seems to be inadequate at this point since it attaches greater value to the state of the being which realizes its potentialities than to the being in the presence of which such potentiality is realized. Only in his final discussion of the happy life of the contemplator does Aristotle, greatest of relational value theorists, indicate the duality of the good —that it is to be found not only in the activity of the contemplative being but also in that object toward which such contemplation is directed and which corresponds to the excellent activity. Objective good, or the value to a subject of that reality other than itself which is necessary to its activity, and subjective good, or the value of increased and perfected activity directed toward good objects, are inseparable from each other. Is Schlick's ethics of kindness concerned with the kindness of fellow men, a kindness which is good for the man with a capacity for happiness, or is it concerned with the kindness of this ethical subject, good to his fellow men? He gives us no adequate answer, but seems to be concerned with both; yet the two are evidently distinct goods. Consistent relational value

[1] In an excellent critique of this essay as originally published, Prof. George Schrader seems to have missed the point I am trying to make here and so to have been misled elsewhere in interpreting my thought. (Cf. George Schrader, "Value and Valuation," in *Faith and Ethics*, 1957, pp. 173-204.) Doubtless my statement was inadequate; hence I have revised it somewhat in the hope of clarifying the idea. Since others also may encounter difficulties in understanding what I am trying to say I shall point out I do not wish to maintain that there is value in the self's relation to itself (or to its potential self) apart from its relation to others. The self's growth in intelligence, kindness, integrity, etc. is doubtless good or these are goods, i.e., virtues; but their goodness is primarily their goodness for other selves; secondarily, they are good-for-the-self as social being dependent not only on approval but on service of others. It is highly questionable for me whether we can call the virtues good in the self apart from their goodness for other selves or for the community of selves. The theory of value I am seeking to present is through and through social; I know of no self-relatedness apart from other-relatedness or self-alienation apart from alienation from the other. Potentiality in the whole realm of being is an important component in the situation in which there is value but the basis of this relational value theory is not the relation of existence to essence, it is that of self to other. Philosophically, it is more indebted to G. H. Mead than to Aristotle; theologically, it is closer, I believe, to Jonathan Edwards ("consent of being to being") than to Thomas Aquinas.

theory will keep in mind that value in the sense of that which is good-for a subject always includes two kinds of worth which may be conveniently designated as external goods and internal goods and that these cannot be separated from each other in activity though they can and must be recognized in their distinctness.

Relational value theory, to be complete, holds together, while it distinguishes, these three relations: first, the relation of an existent being to other existent beings which are its objective or external or complementary goods; second, the relation of the existent being to its own essence, its internal or subjective good; and third, the relation of the movement of the being toward the former good to its movement toward the latter. Even so the situation in which good appears and can be analyzed has not been completely described, for the existent being which is becoming what it is potentially and which meets such complementary good in its environment, is itself good-for the other beings (if not bad-for them) and it forms a part of larger complexes of being, as when men live in society, or animals participate in the evolutionary process of life. These also are on their way to becoming what they are in essence. Thus relational value theory is concerned with a great multi-dimensionality of value, which is not the multi-dimensionality of an abstract realm of essential values but rather the multi-dimensionality of beings in their relations to each other.

Such relational value theory is then relativistic, not in the sense that value is relative to emotion, hence private and irrational, but in the sense in which physical science is relativistic without loss of objectivity. Though this relativism raises great problems of its own, it offers intelligible answers to many of the questions which vex absolute and subjective value theories. The problem of the relation of value to being does not need to be answered in the paradoxical fashion in which intuitionists and emotionalists leave it. The former having defined value as *sui generis*, distinct from existence, tend almost inevitably, it seems, to confuse it then with a certain kind of being, that of the ideas for instance, and at the same time to deny value to nonideal existence. They quickly confuse good with the idea of good and the latter with the goodness of ideas. The bifurcation between being and value becomes identified with the bifurcation of being into essence and existence, or of idea and power. The prejudice in such value theories for the goodness of the spiritual as opposed to the material, and for the goodness of the nonexistent as opposed to the existent, involves them in many consequent difficulties to which the history of ethics bears ample witness.

On the other hand, the equally or more extreme disjunction between value and being which appears in the subjectivisms that regard good as a function of desire, relating value to only one sort of power and that an ultimately unintelligible one, results in the irrationality of separating value judgments from fact judgments. It is an irrational result since it leaves value judgments beyond the range of rational criticism and ignores the presence of value judgments in all fact judgments. Those who demand the substitution of scientific method in ethics for the emotional value judgments which are said to prevail are actually operating with a prior value judgment which they do not acknowledge or criticize, namely, the assertion that knowledge is the greatest good for man. Moreover, they ignore and leave uncriticized the presence of value judgments in every factual judgment which asserts that some factors in a given situation are more important or significant than others.

Relational value theory understands that being and value are inseparably connected but that value cannot be identified with a certain mode of being or any being considered in isolation, whether it be ideal or actual. Value is present wherever being confronts being, wherever there is becoming in the midst of plural, interdependent, and interacting existences. It is not a function of being as such but of being in relation to being. It is therefore universal, co-extensive with the realm of being, and yet not identifiable with any being, even universal being. For if anything existed simply in itself and by itself, value would not be present. Value is the good-for-ness of being for being in their reciprocity, their animosity, and their mutual aid. Value cannot be defined or intuited in itself for it has no existence in itself; and nothing is valuable in itself, but everything has value, positive or negative, in its relations. Thus value is not a relation but arises in the relations of being to being.

On the basis of relational value theory the problem of the knowledge of the good receives a new solution. It is understood that there is an objective element in all such knowledge insofar as an observer stands apart from the being for which another or some future state of its own existence is good. Medical and political judgments about what is good for a physical being or a society can be objective enough, though, of course, they may be mistaken. Yet no being, no self at least, realizes the goodness of the good-for-it without desire. So long as a self does not desire a state of being for itself—such as health—and the external goods which are necessary for that state of being; or so long as it does not desire the presence of a being external to itself as its good—such as a true science or a friend—and that state of its own being which is necessary for the apprehension of that external good; so long it fails to recognize the good as its good. It is as blind to its good as without visual perception it would be blind to objects. Yet desire uncriticized by a rational nonpartici-pating, disinterested view of the relations of being to being is as subject to error as is sensation without rational interpretation. The "blooming and buzzing confusion" of sensation unorganized by ra-tional pattern is no greater than the vagueness, confusion, and inde-terminacy of desire reaching out for it knows not what. A version of the Kantian observation seems applicable in connection with the knowledge of value: "Desire without reason is blind; reason without desire is impotent." There is no rational knowledge of value without rational empirical knowledge of the beings for which others and states of itself are valuable; but the rational knowledge of value is inadequate to move a being toward its own goods. Beliefs about the good-for-me may be true; they do not become effective until the good-for-me becomes the object of desire.

Again relational value theory can distinguish between the good and the right without reducing the one to the other or setting up two independent principles. "Right" means that relation between beings, good-for-each-other, in which their potentiality of being good for each other is realized. It is that relation in which beings that are actually bound together in their interdependent existence con-sent to each other, actually further each other, in the realization of their potentialities. It indeed becomes a part of the good as when the right relation of citizens to each other in a society becomes component to the goodness of that society for other societies or as when the right relations between emotion and reason in an indi-vidual become component to his goodness for his fellow men.

But, in the interaction of being with being, right is not merely a means to the good; it is the goodness of relatedness in action. It is never definable in the abstract but only by reference to the nature and the relations of beings in interaction. The "ought" in which the sense of right comes to expression is a statement of what is owed to another being. It has significance in such a sentence as "A man ought to pay his debts to his creditors," since he is bound to his creditors in an actual community of interdependent life. What significance it has in such a sentence as "Justice ought to be," is hard to discern. Even truth carries obligation with it because it is a relation between beings, specifically between persons, who are bound to each other in communication and who owe each other the truth because they are values and disvalues to each other. Apart from the interrelation of beings having value and disvalue for each other, "right" and "ought" are probably meaningless terms. Yet to confine the term "right" to that situation in which a being seeks a state of itself as its end and uses various external goods as means to the achievement of this end is to ignore the multiplicity of value relations. The "right" is coextensive with the realm of interdependent values, that is, of interdependent beings.

Though relational value theory is actually widely employed even where it is not acknowledged and though it offers solutions to problems which remain insoluble by means of other hypotheses about the nature of the good, yet it is regarded with understandable suspicion by men who are profoundly concerned not only about truth in human society but also about other kinds of right relations between human beings and between these and the nonhuman environment. Though relational value theory is not psychologically relativistic it is evidently dogmatically relativistic since it is necessary to take one's standpoint with or in some being accepted as the *center of value* if one is to construct anything like a consistent system of value judgments and determinations of what is right. The difficulty becomes apparent in the essentially relationist, though apparently psychological, theories of English empiricism. The continuing concern of this empiricism was the substitution of a "realistic" for traditional ethics. It sought to move legislators and citizens to answer the questions, "What is really good for man?" and "What is really good for society?" on the basis of an understanding of human needs and potentialities rather than by reference to established maxims. Its frequent definition of man as fundamentally a pleasure-seeking creature or as economic man interested in and in need of material goods was evidently too narrow for its own use, since, at least implicitly, it recognized his social nature, his need for other men as good-for-him and his reflective nature, his recognition of his good-for-ness in relation to others and his society.

Its real problem, however, seemed to center in its recognition that there were two dogmatic starting points for its inquiry. On the one hand it was individualistic, making the individual person the center of value and inquiring what was good for him. From this point of view it required of society that it make all its judgments about good and right by reference to the needs of individuals in their process of becoming. Its hedonistic subjectivism was translated, as in utilitarianism, into objective relationism. The legislator was not expected to ask, "What is good for me?" but rather, "What is good for the individual citizens?" On the other hand, this empiricism was aware of another value-center, the society. Here was a continuing existence, the English community, and the question from this point of view was, "What is good for this society?" Between these two objective but relativistic value systems English ethics sought to find some kind of reconciliation but never with complete success.

Another dogmatic relativism appeared when life itself was made the value-center by evolutionary ethics and it appeared that questions could be significantly raised about the good-for-life. Further, the dogmatic nature of every starting point came to consciousness in the questions easily brushed aside but not easily forgotten about the kind of value system which fish or ants might construct if they could consciously make themselves, as individuals or as communities, the centers of value. So it seems that on the basis of an objective but relativistic value theory there can be as many theoretical value systems as there are beings in existence. Yet none of these relative systems is relativistic in the sense of being dependent on feeling or desire; each can be objective in the sense that it may be a system dealing with actual value relations and in the sense that the value judgments made within that frame of reference are subject to critical inquiry into their truth or falsity.

In view of this necessity of beginning with a value-center it seems evident that every theory of value, so far as it is relational, is religious in character. Every such theory adopts as its explicit or implicit starting point some being or beings in relation to which good is judged to be good and evil evil, in relation to which also the rightness or wrongness of its relations to other beings is examined. The question of the goodness of this central being for other beings is usually not considered, as when in the relational value-thinking of an Aristotle the question about man's goodness for other beings is not raised; the beginning and the end of his ethics is man.

Thus also vitalistic or evolutionary value systems beginning with life or the community of living beings can make rational judgments about what is good for life—the fitness of an environment, the mutual limitation of living beings in right relations of the struggle for existence—but it cannot or does not raise the question what the community of the living is good for. Sometimes a single value, such as knowledge, is deified as the value-center about the goodness of which for other valuable beings no one inquires, though more often duality of deity seems to be posited here as when science is regarded as the great good for man and man is thought of as the servant of knowledge, whose meaning lies in his service to science. More frequently the relational value theories, implicit or explicit in purportedly objective or subjective theories, are caught up in a polytheism which posits two or more centers of values. So on the one hand Hartmann presents us with a kind of Epicurean faith in which the center of value is the realm of ideal essences which have their being above the world of existences in self-sufficiency, yet so that only in relation to them anything else has value. On the other hand man is his center of value, in relation to whom even the ideas of value alone have actual worth. Or the polytheism is that of human society and the human individual and the community of living beings as centers of value which must somehow be reconciled.

Although Christian and Jewish theologies have often identified themselves in their value-thinking with objective and spiritualistic theories of value, relational value theory is much more compatible with their fundamental outlook and much more in line with the realism of their reverence for being. Its relativism, when recognized, agrees with their concern that relative things should be kept relative and never confused with the transcendent absolute. Its realism, that is, its solid founding of value on the nature of being, agrees with their conviction that the starting point of all inquiry lies in the recognition of *that which is*. The objections which they raise to relational value-thinking are not directed toward its rational relativism but against its tendency to fall into a psychological relativism for which "there is nothing either good or bad but thinking makes it so," and against the unconquerable tendency to absolutize some relative starting point such as man, or society, or ideas, or life. Dogma, doubtless, there must be, since the analysis even of value cannot begin in the void but must start with an act of decision for some being as value-center. But the dogmatism of a relativism which assumes the privileged position of one finite reality, such as man, is so narrow that it cuts off inquiry into great realms of value, and tends to confine the discussion of the good to an arbitrarily chosen field, for instance to that of the human good.

For the polytheistic theologies of value, usually called philosophical, which confine themselves to two or three of these relative systems, and then become involved in questions about their interrelations, monotheistic faith substitutes, first, a central value theory and then the recognition of an infinite number of possible, relative value systems. Its starting point, its dogmatic beginning, is with the transcendent One for whom alone there is an ultimate good and for whom, as the source and end of all things, whatever is, is good. It may indeed use a sort of psychological relativism at this point, since it cannot say that God has need of any being external to himself; hence it may be able only to say that whatever is exists because it pleases God. But whether the relation is to need or to desire, in any case the starting point is that transcendent absolute for whom, or for which, whatever is, is good. Such faith no more begins by asking what God is good for than humanistic or vitalistic ethics begins with the inquiry what man or life is good for. But it has the great advantage over humanism and vitalism that it does not offer an evident abstraction of one sort of finite being from the rest of existence with the consequent appearance of arbitrariness in the selection of finite centers of value that from any disinterested point of view have no greater claim to centrality than any others.

With this beginning the value theory of monotheistic theology is enabled to proceed to the construction of many relative value systems, each of them tentative, experimental, and objective, as it considers the interaction of beings on beings, now from the point of view of man, now from the point of view of society, now from the point of view of life. But it is restrained from erecting any one of these into an absolute, or even from ordering it above the others, as when the human-centered value system is regarded as superior to a life-centered system. A monotheistically centered value theory is not only compatible with such objective relativism in value analysis but requires it in view of its fundamental dogma that none is absolute save God and that the absolutizing of anything finite is ruinous to the finite itself.

There is room within the objective relativism of monotheistic faith for the recognition of the value of ideal essences for minds, and of minds for ideal essences, but none for the absolutizing of such essences or such minds as good in themselves. There is room here for the recognition of the value of man for the ongoing community of life and vice versa, but none for the dogmatic choice of life or man as the absolute centers of value. When it turns to human ethics theocentric value theory inevitably will become relatively man-centered, yet tentatively so and never with forgetfulness of the question of what man is good for in his relations not only to the transcendent One but also to the other existent beings.

Hence it is not monotheistic faith that is uncritically dogmatic in its construction of value theories. Uncritical dogmatism is the practice of those explicit or disguised relational systems of thought about the good which arbitrarily choose some limited starting point for their inquiries and either end with the confession that value is an irrational concept which must nevertheless be rationally employed because nature requires this, or otherwise rule out of consideration great realms of value relations as irrelevant. Critical thought based on theocentric faith has no quarrel with the *method* of objective relativism in value theory and ethics. It objects only but strongly to the religious foundations of these relativisms.

III

*Faith in Gods and in God**

THERE is nothing distinctive or peculiar about a Protestant's interest in the ultimate theological problem. We are concerned with the questions of God's nature and existence not as Protestants or Catholics, Christians or Jews, theologians or philosophers, laymen or clergy, but simply as human beings. Yet each of us raises these problems in a specific form, each asks his question in that special way which he has not only learned from his tradition, but which has been made necessary by his own personal wrestling with the question of life's meaning. Hence we often quarrel about the answers we get to our questions without realizing that they are answers to different questions. And sometimes we quarrel about our questions, maintaining that our way of asking is the only significant way; that our problem is the only meaningful one. So the philosopher of religion may begin with a certain definition of the term "God" and then ask, "Does a being having this nature exist?" This is a perfectly legitimate question. But it is wrong to think of it as the only proper way of raising the problem. Many different definitions of the nature of God may be framed, and hence many problems of existence may be raised; and the contention about the answers may simply be contention about the social meaning of a word, a matter on which we ought to be able to come to an agreement easily were it not for the emotional and sentimental attachment we have to certain words. The question about God may be raised in a wholly different way, in the manner of the metaphysician who asks, "What is the ultimate nature of reality, or what is the first cause, what the final end, what the nature of the primal energy, what are the attributes of substance?" Here we have a different series of questions, and the relation of the answers given to them to the answers given to the question whether "God" exists is not immedi-

* Essay entitled "The Nature and Existence of God" from *Motive*, December 1943.

ately apparent. If the term "God" is used in this latter, metaphysical type of inquiry, it is not to be taken for granted that the word has the same reference, the same meaning, which it has in the former type.

It is important, first of all, to recognize that each of us raises the question about "God" in a specific way, that it is necessary for us to phrase our question as sharply as we can, to seek an answer to that particular question and to avoid the defensiveness which makes us regard our question, just because it is ours, as more important than anyone else's. We need also, of course, to avoid the feeling that our question is unimportant because others have other questions. As a Protestant theologian or as a man who seeks to understand what he believes with the aid of Protestant theology, I do not raise the question of God in the way the philosopher of religion or the metaphysician does; while I cannot maintain that my way of asking is superior to theirs, neither can I be easily convinced that my question is illegitimate, that it is not a true, human, and important question.

It appears that the different methods we employ in religious inquiry are not wholly unlike the different methods used in science. Though all scientists are interested in truth they do not raise the question about truth in the abstract, but ask specific questions, such as those which psychologists on the one hand, physicists on the other, natural scientists on the one hand, social scientists on the other, raise and attempt to answer. Each scientist, doubtless, tends to think that his question and mode of inquiry is the most important, yet he learns eventually to live in a certain democracy of science, wherein he maintains his right to seek truth in a specific way without requiring all others to abandon their specific inquiries and to join him in his search. In some such fashion I conceive Protestant theology at work. It is well aware of other inquirers in the same general field and it profits greatly by counsel and debate with them. Yet it seeks to remain true to its own particular problem and to its own method of inquiry.

How, then, does Protestantism raise the question of God and how does it seek and find its answers to its problems? How does the problem of God present itself to us who work in this living tradition? It comes to us as an eminently practical problem, a problem of human existence and destiny, of the meaning of human life in general and of the life of self and its community in particular. It does not arise for us in the speculative form of such questions as "Does God exist?" or "What is the first cause, what the ultimate substance?" Our first question is *How is faith in God possible?* In other words, the problem of God arises for us in its subjective rather than objective, or, better, in personal rather than impersonal form. (That we are exposed to certain great dangers in consequence —to solipsism, for instance—is evident but every inquiry involves particular dangers and the possibility of particular errors.) This seems to be the way in which the great Protestant thinkers— Luther, Calvin, Edwards, Schleiermacher, Kierkegaard—and that philosopher who is most Protestant of all philosophers, Kant—raised the question about God primarily. It is also the way in which Protestantism as a religious movement has approached the religious problem of the ordinary man. It has not sought to convince a speculative, detached mind of the existence of God, but has begun with actual moral and religious experience, with the practical reasoning of the existing person rather than with the speculative interests of a detached mind.

1. WHAT IS FAITH?

The point at which such Protestants begin their analysis of the problem of God is that of practical human faith in deity. Such faith may be described in various ways, but it is never correctly described when it is initially defined in terms of intellectual belief. The belief that something exists is an experience of a wholly different order from the experience of reliance on it. The faith we speak of in Protestantism and of which, it seems to us, the classic book of Christianity, the Bible, speaks, is not intellectual assent to the truth of certain propositions, but a personal, practical trusting in, reliance on, counting upon something. So we have faith in democracy not insofar as we believe that democracy exists, but insofar as we rely upon the democratic idea or spirit to maintain itself and to influence the lives of people continuously. We have faith in the people not insofar as we believe in the existence of such a reality as "the people" but insofar as we count upon the character of what we call the people to manifest itself steadfastly in the maintenance of certain values. Faith, in other words, always refers primarily to character and power rather than to existence. Existence is implied and necessarily implied; but there is no direct road from assent to the intellectual proposition that something exists to the act of confidence and reliance upon it. Faith is an active thing, a committing of self to something, an anticipation. It is directed toward something that is also active, that has power or is power. It is distinguished from belief both on its subjective side and with respect to that to which it refers. For belief as assent to the truth of propositions does not necessarily involve reliance in action on that which is believed, and it refers to propositions rather than, as faith does, to agencies and powers.

Now it is evident, when we inquire into ourselves and into our common life, that without such active faith or such reliance and confidence on power we do not and cannot live. Not only the just but also the unjust, insofar as they live, live by faith. We live by knowledge also, it is true, but not by knowledge without faith. In order to know we must always rely on something we do not know; in order to walk by sight we need to rely on what we do not see. The most evident example of that truth is to be found in science, which conducts its massive campaign against obscurity and error on the basis of a great faith in the intelligibility of things; when it does not know and finds hindrances in the path of knowledge, it asserts with stubborn faith that knowledge nevertheless is possible, that there is pattern and intelligibility in the things which are not yet intelligible. Such faith is validated in practice, yet it evermore outruns practice. Our social life, also, proceeds from moment to moment on the ground of a confidence we have in each other which is distinct from our belief in each other's existence and distinct also from our knowledge of each other's character, though such belief and such knowledge do form the background and the foreground of our faith. How much we live by faith in this area becomes apparent to us when we are deceived or betrayed by those on whom we have relied. When treaties are broken, when bankers embezzle, when marriage partners become disloyal, when friends betray, then doubt of all things invades our minds and we understand how much we have lived by reliance on our fellow men. But we also discover that without some confidence which goes beyond our knowledge we cannot exist at all since we are social persons who cannot live in isolation, and that we are ignorant persons who must in all their living go far beyond their knowledge of each other if they would live at all.

When we inquire into this element of faith or confidence in our life as human beings we become aware of one aspect of it which may above all else be called religious, because it is related to our existence as worshiping beings, even as our faith in the intelligibility of nature is related to our existence as knowing beings and our confidence in each other is related to our moral life. This is the faith that life is worth living, or better, the reliance on certain centers of value as able to bestow significance and worth on our existence. It is a curious and inescapable fact about our lives, of which I think we all become aware at some time or another, that we cannot live without a cause, without some object of devotion, some center of worth, something on which we rely for our meaning. In this sense all men have faith because they are men and cannot help themselves, just as they must and do have some knowledge of their world, though their knowledge be erroneous.

The universality of such religious faith is obscured for us. For one thing, we tend in highly institutionalized societies, such as our own, to confuse the reality of human processes with their institutional organization and expression. So we have a tendency to think of schools, laboratories, books, and teachers when we speak of education. Doubtless this institutional education is very important but we need again and again to be made aware of the fact that the actual process of conditioning human minds, of equipping them with the instruments of words and ideas, of giving them an orientation in the world, of transmitting a tradition and developing latent possibilities, goes far beyond the schools and can go on even without the aid of official education. The political process, also, whereby men are governed and govern each other, whereby power is balanced against power, goes on in our community even when the official agencies of politics, the institutionalized forms, are not present. It is so with religion and religious faith and worship. We tend to confuse these with the official organizations and habits, with observance of special rites, with the functioning of a special leadership, and with the expression of a specific faith. But religion is a much more various thing. And it is inescapable as institutions of religion are not. As the faith that life is worth living, as the reference of life to a source of meaning and value, as the practice of adoration and worship, it is common to all men. For no man lives without living for some purpose, for the glorification of some god, for the advancement of some cause. If we do not wish to call this faith religion, there is no need to contend about the word. Let us say then that our problem is the problem of faith rather than of religion.

Now to have faith and to have a god is one and the same thing, as it is one and the same thing to have knowledge and an object of knowledge. When we believe that life is worth living by the same act we refer to some being which makes our life worth living. We never merely believe that life is worth living, but always think of it as made worth living by something on which we rely. And this being, whatever it be, is properly termed our god.

2. Who Is God?

We arrive, then, at the problem of deity by setting out from the universal human experience of faith, of reliance or trust in something. Luther expressed this idea long ago when he asked, "What does it mean to have a god, or what is God?" and answered his question by saying, "Trust and faith of the heart alone make both God and idol. . . . For the two, faith and God, hold close together. Whatever then thy heart clings to . . . and relies upon, that is properly thy God."

Now if this be true, that the word "god" means the object of human faith in life's worthwhileness, it is evident that men have many gods, that our natural religion is polytheistic. (It is also evident that there can be no such thing as an actual atheist though there may be many who profess atheism.) Whatever be our relation to the official monotheism of our religious institutions, the private faith by which we live is likely to be a multifarious thing with many objects of devotion and worship. The most common object of devotion on which we depend for our meaning and value is the self. We tend in human life to a kind of religious Narcissism whereby we make ourselves the most admired of all beings and seek to interpret the meaning of all experiences by reference to their meaning for the central self. The self becomes the center of value and at the same time the being which is to guarantee its own life against meaninglessness, worthlessness, and the threat of frustration.

But this self is never an adequate god for a self. We are forced to recognize that many things bring satisfaction into our lives from the outside, as it were, and we are so interdependent on all the beings about us that we inevitably admire, adore, and look to others as sources of value and meaning to ourselves. Hence we live not only for our own sakes but for the sake of other persons. It is not a figure of speech but a truth that mothers make gods out of their sons and daughters, that the home is the god of all men to a certain extent, since they live for the sake of that home, labor for it and adore it in many an hour of private devotion. One of the most powerful gods of all times, of primitive as of civilized periods, is sex which is represented by many symbols, for the sake of which, and for the enjoyment of which men live. Beyond the dark powers, the Chthonian deities of the physical life of man, there are our Olympian gods—our country, our ideologies, our democracies, civilizations, churches, our art which we practice for art's sake, our truth which we pursue for truth's sake, our moral values, our ideas and the social forces which we personalize, adore, and on which we depend for deliverance from sheer nothingness and the utter inconsequence of existence.

One does not need to draw too sharp a line between personal and institutional religion at this point, as though personal religion were by and large polytheistic while institutional religion is monotheistic. It would be difficult to make out a strong case for the actual monotheism of institutional faith. For instance, one of the beings on which institutionalized faith relies for deliverance from meaninglessness is religion itself.

We note that these centers of value, these objects of adoration, have many different forms of existence. Some are visible and tangible objects of whose reality our senses give us assurance. Some are essences, ideas, concepts, or images which are accessible only to abstract thought, but which exercise a certain compulsion over the mind. Some are movements known only by a kind of empathy or by an intuition that outruns sense; some have the peculiar and hard-to-define reality of selves or persons. But in some sense they all exist.

Yet this is true—and this constitutes the tragedy of our religious life—that none of these values or centers of value exists universally, or can be object of a universal faith. None of them can guarantee meaning to our life in the world save for a time. They are all finite in time as in space and make finite claims upon us. Hence we become aware of two characteristics of our faith and its gods: that we are divided within ourselves and socially by our religion, and that our gods are unable to save us from the ultimate frustration of meaningless existence.

Sometimes we speak of our internal division as though it were caused by the incompleteness of reason's domination over the more primitive desires which are rooted in our physical constitution. But then we realize that we do not desire as primitives or as animals do, but with a passion that indicates how great an investment we have made in the objects of desire. We note also that the life of reason is not without its desire and devotion. We become aware of the truth that our internal divisions are due to a diversity of religious attachments. We look to the objects of the mind for meaning, but we cannot make our physical existence meaningful by our attention and devotion to truth. Our inner conflicts seem due to the fact that we have many sources of value, and that these cannot all be served. Our social conflicts also always have religious character. We cannot and do not fight our wars simply for the sake of maintaining our physical existence. We always appeal to values for the sake of which we live and without which we think that life would not be worth living. We battle for America and England and Germany, which give worth to our lives, and not simply for ourselves. We fight for liberty or solidarity, for equality or for order, for fraternity in a large or in a narrow sense. But none of these gods is universal, and therefore devotion to one always implies exclusion of another. So the gods are divisive socially as well as within the person.

In this situation we dream of integration, of a great pantheon in which all the gods will be duly served, each in its proper sphere. So we speak sometimes of establishing a new synthesis of civilization, of the integration of personality, of the recognition of a great hierarchy of values. But the synthesis is never achieved, the integration never worked out. For each god in turn requires a certain absolute devotion and the denial of the claims of the other gods. So long as country seems an absolute source of value to us, so long devotion to one country will make us deny the claims of every other. So long as we pursue art for art's sake, so long art will be the enemy of morality and of truth. The best we can achieve in this realm is a sort of compromise among many absolute claims. We remain beings, therefore, with many faiths held in succession. We practice a kind of successive polygamy, being married now to this and now to that object of devotion.

The tragedy of our religious life is not only that it divides us within ourselves and from each other. There is a greater tragedy— the twilight of the gods. None of these beings on which we rely to give content and meaning to our lives is able to supply continuous meaning and value. The causes for which we live all die. The great social movements pass and are supplanted by others. The ideals we fashion are revealed by time to be relative. The empires and cities to which we are devoted all decay. At the end nothing is left to defend us against the void of meaninglessness. We try to evade this knowledge, but it is ever in the background of our minds. The apocalyptic vision of the end of all things assails us, whether we see that end as the prophets of the pre-Christian era did or as the pessimists of our time do. We know that "on us and all our race the slow, sure doom falls pitiless and dark." All our causes, all our ideas, all the beings on which we relied to save us from worthlessness are doomed to pass.

3. GOD

What is it that is responsible for this passing, that dooms our human faith to frustration? We may call it the nature of things, we may call it fate, we may call it reality. But by whatever name we call it, this law of things, this reality, this way things are, is something with which we all must reckon. We may not be able to give a name to it, calling it only the "void" out of which everything comes and to which everything returns, though that is also a name. But it is there—the last shadowy and vague reality, the secret of existence by virtue of which things come into being, are what they are, and pass away. Against it there is no defense. This reality, this nature of things, abides when all else passes. It is the source of all things and the end of all. It surrounds our life as the great abyss into which all things plunge and as the great source whence they all come. What it is we do not know save that it is and that it is the supreme reality with which we must reckon.

Now a strange thing has happened in our history and in our personal life; our faith has been attached to that great void, to that enemy of all our causes, to that opponent of all our gods. The strange thing has happened that we have been enabled to say of this reality, this last power in which we live and move and have our being, "Though it slay us yet will we trust it." We have been allowed to attach our confidence to it, and put our reliance in it which is the one reality beyond all the many, which is the last power, the infinite source of all particular beings as well as their end. And insofar as our faith, our reliance for meaning and worth, has been attached to this source and enemy of all our gods, we have been enabled to call this reality God.

Let us raise three questions about this fact that faith has become attached to the void and to the enemy which surrounds our life. The first one is, What does it mean to attach faith to this power? The second, How does such faith come about? And the third, What are the consequences of such faith?

First, to have faith in this reality means that, having been driven away from our reliance on all the lesser causes, we have learned to conceive of and to rely upon this last power, this nature of things, as itself the greatest of all causes, the undefeatable cause. We have learned to say, "For this cause was I born and therefore I came into the world that I might make glorious the name and exhibit the power of this last cause." And we have been enabled to say it with satisfaction, with love and hope and confidence; for to have faith in something as able to give value to our lives is to love it. Without such love there is no faith. And to have faith is also to live in hope, in constant anticipation of new unfoldings of worth and meaning.

To attach faith, hope, and love to this last being, this source of all things and this slayer of all, is to have confidence which is not subject to time, for this is the eternal reality, this is the last power. It is to have a love for that which is not exclusive but inclusive, since this reality, this great X, is the source of all things and the end of all. It is, therefore, to be put into the position of those who can love all things in him or in it, and who deny all things in it. "It is a consoling idea," wrote Kierkegaard, "that before God we are always in the wrong." All the relative judgments of worth are equalized in the presence of this One who loves all and hates all, but whose love like whose hatred is without emotion, without favoritism. To have hope of this One is to have hope that is eternal. This being cannot pass away. And to hope for the manifestations of his judgments and his love is to hope to eternity.

When we conceive faith in this one, our foundations have indeed been laid in despair, not in the grandiloquent despair of *A Free Man's Worship*, but in the sober despair which has faced the reality of the death of all things and the endlessness of the creative process.

Another way of describing this faith is one which I have learned from Professor Whitehead's little book on religion. Religion, he says, "is transition from God the void to God the enemy, and from

God the enemy to God the companion."[1] When we say that we conceive faith in the great void and the great enemy we mean that we have learned to count on it as friend. We have learned to rely on it as a cause to which we may devote our lives, as that which will make all our lives and the lives of all things valuable even though it bring them to death.

Second, how is such a faith possible? How does it happen that this void, this enemy, is recognized as friend, that faith attaches itself to the last power, to the great hidden mystery, and calls it God, that man can lose himself in adoration of this being, saying with the Psalmist, "Whom have I in heaven but thee? and there is none upon earth that I desire beside thee?" or with Job, "Though he slay me, yet will I trust in him"?

It has happened in our human history and it does happen in personal histories. Men may dispute endlessly about the worth of that happening, though when they do they always do so on the basis of another faith than faith in this God. But there can be no doubt of the fact that it has happened and that it does happen.

How does it happen to the individual? It does not happen without the struggle of his reason. For by reason he discovers the inadequacy of all his gods and is driven to despair in life's meaning. It does not happen without experience, without the experience of frustration, of noting the death of all things, the experience of the internal division in which his various worship involves him, the experience of the great social catastrophes which show the weakness of the great causes and beings in which he trusted as saviors of life. It does not happen without the operation of something we must call spiritual, something which is like the intuition of the thinker, like the creative insight of the artist, like the flash of recognition of truth. All these elements are involved. Furthermore, this transfer of faith to the ultimate being does not take place without moral struggle, without recognition of the unworthiness both of our transgressions and our obediences to our moral laws.

But for most men another element is involved—the concrete meeting with other men who have received this faith, and the concrete meeting with Jesus Christ. There may be other ways, but this is the usual way for us, that we confront in the event of Jesus Christ the presence of that last power which brings to apparent nothingness the life of the most loyal man. Here we confront the slayer, and

[1] A. N. Whitehead, *Religion in the Making*, 1926, pp. 16 f.

here we become aware that this slayer is the life-giver. He does not put to shame those who trust in him. In the presence of Jesus Christ we most often conceive, or are given that faith. We may try to understand how we might have received the faith without Jesus Christ; but the fact remains that when this faith was given Jesus Christ was there.

So it is in history. This faith in the One has had its occasional manifestations elsewhere. But it has happened in history that it has been conceived and received where a people who regarded themselves as chosen suffered the most cruel fate, and where a Son of man who was obedient to death actually suffered death. Here the great reconciliation with the divine enemy has occurred. And since it has occurred, there is no way of getting rid of it. It is in our human history.

We do not say that this faith in the last power is something men ought to have. We say only this, that it is the end of the road of faith, that it is unassailable, and that when men receive it they receive a great gift. We say that it is given, that it has been given, that it is being given, and that when it is received very profound consequences follow.

Third, the consequences of faith in the one, final, and only God are not automatic, for faith involves the whole person, and the gift of faith is not a possession which we can hold in our power. It is something that lives in man and by which man lives. It is not a possession which can be held fast in the form of a creed. It is a basis for all thinking, but though it may be expressed in the form of a thought, it is not itself a thought; it is the reliance of a person on a person. Beginning with that faith life is involved intellectually and morally in a continuous revolution.

This faith opens the way to knowledge. It removes the taboos which surround our intellectual life, making some subjects too holy to be inquired into and some too dangerous for us to venture into. Yet it grants reverence to the mind for which now no being is too low to be worthy of a loving curiosity. All knowledge becomes reverent and all being is open to inquiry. So long as we try to maintain faith in the gods, we fear to examine them too closely lest their relativity in goodness and in power become evident, as when Bible worshipers fear Biblical criticism, or democracy worshipers fear objective examination of democracy. But when man's faith is attached to the One, all relative beings may be received at his hands for nurture and for understanding. Understanding is not automatically given with faith; faith makes possible and demands the labor of the intellect that it may understand.

The moral consequences of this faith is that it makes relative all those values which polytheism makes absolute, and so puts an end to the strife of the gods. But it does not relativize them as self-love does. A new sacredness attaches to the relative goods. Whatever is, is now known to be good, to have value, though its value be still hidden to us. The moral consequences of faith in God is the universal love of all being in him. It is not an automatic consequence. Faith is never so complete that it is not accompanied by self-defensiveness. But this is its requirement: that all beings, not only our friends but also our enemies, not only men but also animals and the inanimate, be met with reverence, for all are friends in the friendship of the one to whom we are reconciled in faith.

So faith in God involves us in a permanent revolution of the mind and of the heart, a continuous life which opens out infinitely into ever new possibilities. It does not, therefore, afford grounds for boasting but only for simple thankfulness. It is a gift of God.

IV

Science in Conflict with Morality?[1]

WHETHER the relation of science to morality—in human life in general and in modern existence particularly—is fairly definable as one of conflict may be questioned. In our time, however, it is at least one of high tension. Perhaps it has always been so; for since the time of Aristotle philosophers have distinguished between the sort of reasoning we do in knowing the objects of the intellect and the kind we do in choosing between important and unimportant, more and less valuable modes of action; and to many of them it has seemed that there is no way of uniting systematically in a single theory these ways of reasoning. Only the individual self that both knows and acts provides an unintellectualizable or at least unconceptualizable unity to these various processes. So long as we deal with them only in theory something like conflict must seem to obtain between that practical reasoning which looks toward final causes or ends, presupposes deliberative freedom of some sort in the agent, distinguishes between good and evil, and that observer's reasoning which looks only to efficient, material, formal, or antecedent causes, which assumes perhaps the presence of chance but abstracts from personal freedom and from all judgments about the goodness or the evil of the actualities and factualities it seeks to understand.

Yet the difficulty of reconciling science and morality is not only theoretic. It appears in its acutest form in the individual and social existence in which both activities are going on. We see it manifesting itself in scientists who find that the results and consequences of their labors are put to uses they cannot approve as men. The movements that led from peaceful studies to the holocaust of Hiroshima

[1] Lecture delivered at St. John's College, Annapolis, Md., Feb. 28, 1959, as part of a symposium on the theme, "The Scientist as Philosopher."

and the paralysis of cold war, from psychological laboratories to brain washings and the manipulation of human emotions so that trivial products might be marketed, from the open doors and free communication of an international science to treason trials and the secrecy of guarded research centers, seem only to have made publicly dramatic a problem that has been evident to morally sensitive scientists for a long time.

In one form or another many a scientist raises the question now as in the past: What is the actual value of all this work that I am doing, what is the meaning of my vocation, what the justification of this activity? The question is a moral question and the answer can no longer be a scientific but is inevitably a moral answer.

Frequently justification is made in the terms of a vitalistic morality that regards life as the highest good; but in a world where the question about the meaning or value of life is widely raised and where knowledge is used for the destruction as well as enhancement of life neither scientists nor their lay companions can long rest content with that answer. Frequently also it is still simply assumed, as from the beginning of science in Greece, that true knowledge is the key value which will unlock the treasuries of all other human goods—such as honesty and justice, courage and kindliness, beauty and peace and whatever else men find praiseworthy. But on the whole disillusionment about these things prevails and has long prevailed. A generation ago Max Weber remarked in his address on "Science as a Vocation," "Who—aside from certain big children who are indeed found in the natural sciences—still believes that the findings of astronomy, biology, physics or chemistry could teach us anything about the *meaning* of the world?" And he goes on to say, "What is the meaning of science as a vocation now after these former illusions, the 'way to true being,' the 'way to true art,' the 'way to true nature,' the 'way to true God,' the 'way to true happiness' have been dispelled?"[2] In this question about the meaning and value of science as a vocation—a question explored significantly by Michael Polanyi in his book *Personal Knowledge*,[3]—the problem of science and morality appears in an acute, but complex form. It is a problem of conflict or of tension within the scientist himself.

The problem arises also, of course, in the development of science

---

[2] Max Weber, *Essays in Sociology*, Translated, Edited and with an Introduction by H. H. Gerth and C. Wright Mills, 1946, pp. 142 and 143.
[3] *Personal Knowledge—Towards a Post-Critical Philosophy*, 1958.

as a social enterprise. The subsidization or coercive enslavement of science to serve ideological national interests, whether in the sphere of democracy or of communism, and the protests of science against such enslavement present us with a moral problem that is not soluble by the methods of science itself. Here is conflict not because morality clashes with science but because one kind of morality is arrayed against another: the morality which places loyalty to society above all other loyalties and the morality for which devotion to true and universal knowledge is the last devotion. May science have achieved emancipation from servitude to dogmatic religion only to fall prey in its later days to the dogmatism of other ideologies or to become a pawn in power struggles in which might not only makes right but truth also?

Or as we think of the confused situation, we may have in mind the problem of science and morality as it appears in the education of the new generations. How shall we nurture our future leaders of society and the citizens of the human republic? Are we not consciously and diligently seeking now to bring forth in them the virtues of *techne* and *episteme*, or of certain other intellectual excellences, while we leave to chance or to the operation of unacknowledged forces the development of their personal moral habits in integrity, justice, courage, and self-control? And has not the preoccupation of our times with true knowledge abandoned to the reign of instinct or of uncriticized social mores the whole realm of existence that does not come under the reign of intellect but rather of what we used to call the "will" but have now ignored so long that like the self itself we have become dubious about its actuality? Often it seems that as light has spread over the objective world in which we live the shadows over our personal life have deepened, so that the period of Enlightenment has become a Dark Age in which we grow more ignorant about ourselves and about good and evil. But when we have begun to reflect along these lines and have been tempted to say that the day of science has become the dark night of the soul of man, we remember how this same science has helped to deliver us from many superstitions about relative goods and evils and from how many bungling, disastrous manifestations of good will unenlightened by right understanding.

I cannot presume to offer any theories that will help us to resolve these puzzles in the relations of observer's and agent's reasonings, of science and morality. To be able to do so I would need to transcend myself as one who as a whole person yet seeks both to know and to do, to be discriminating both in his understanding and his choosing, choosing in order to understand, understanding in order to choose. I would also have had to participate in the work of science as much as I have participated in the work of ethical criticism. But my knowledge of the scientist's work and vocation is wholly a lay, that is an outside, knowledge. Hence all that I can contribute are the reflections of a moral theologian whose work must always be directed toward the effort to increase self-knowledge among men—a task apparently so far removed from the work of the natural scientist that conversation between moralist and scientist sometimes leads not so much to conflict as to the more grievous situation of misunderstanding or total lack of comprehension. Nevertheless I must make my effort to contribute what I can to understanding our puzzling situation as moral men living in a society whose highest achievement is in the work of science. I shall do so by offering my reflections on the morality of science and on the apparent effect of science on the morality of our Western society.

The morality of science is something rather different from the morality of men who devote most of their attention—but never all of it—to scientific inquiry. Doubtless the morality of the study and the laboratory is not without its influence on the evaluations and commitments made in family, cultural society, nation, and church. But just as we must not allow our appreciations of a man's domestic virtues and vices to obscure our understanding and evaluation of his political principles, or vice versa, so we will not confuse the morals of man as scientist with the morals of scientist as whole man. Most of the scientists I know are admirably sensitive to human values and discriminating in their choices as they make political, educational, cultural, and domestic decisions and commitments. Many of them are keenly conscious of aesthetic and religious good and evil. But these qualities of moral discrimination they share with men of other vocations in our society. It is not evident that their moral sensitiveness is a function of their scientific activity, and so it is not with this general morality, with its scale of values and its sense of obligation, that I am now concerned.

Neither shall I mean by the morality of science the explicit moral philosophy of scientists. Strangely enough while not a few of them, particularly in the most advanced natural sciences, have developed epistemological and metaphysical or ontological reflections —more or less on the basis of their science—not many seem to have turned to consistent reflection on the ethics of their scientific activity or on ethics as related to such activity. There are exceptions, such as Michael Polyani, and Max Weber; doubtless greater familiarity with the literature of science would lead to further qualification of the statement. But by and large science seems conditioned by the very nature of its activity to look in an outward direction, toward what is objective whether in the form of phenomena or of theory; hence it seems not to reflect much on its own activity except as this is related to what is before it. Hence also even discussions of scientific method rarely yield much direct insight into the *ethos* of the scientific enterprise. The situation in science seems at this point to be akin to the situation in art. Not many great artists seem to have communicated their reflections on the meaning, the values, and the disciplines of their work. They seem to say what they have to say in their objective works. The interpreter of the inward aspects of artistic activity must try to re-enact as best he can the evaluations, decisions, and commitments of artists, their struggles with truth and falseness, with integrity and temptation to deceit. Scientist like artist in his own activity seems always to be involved in moral choices but his vocation does not bring these into the focus of his attention; he does not often speak of them. They are, however, the subject matter of the moralist.

When the latter looks at science he becomes aware first of all perhaps of the *commitment* which is involved in the role or office of a scientist. He sees that this science, as the common enterprise of a community and as the particular activity of individuals, is maintained not only by the wonder or curiosity or desire for power which may have given it its first impetus but by a kind of sworn loyalty to a cause. There is something somewhat amusing to him when he encounters in a book on science which has argued that all ethical statements are arbitrary, emotional, and purely volitional—not subject to judgments of their truth and falseness—a statement such as the following: "A scientific philosophy cannot supply moral guidance; that is one of its results and cannot be held against it. You want the truth, and nothing but the truth? Then do not ask

---

4 Hans Reichenbach, *The Rise of Scientific Philosophy*, 1951, p. 323.

the philosopher for moral directives."[4] What is amusing to him about such a statement is that it contains moral advice and invites to moral decision in the very expression of the impossibility of giving advice. What it says, to me at least, is this: Science is an enterprise committed to the search for truth, or for true knowledge; now if you want to be a scientist you must devote yourself to that one good end and not expect to get advice from those so committed on how to achieve other human ends, such as justice or true happiness. Is not that moral advice, advice about ends to be pursued and about the consequences of such devotion?

The morality of science is the morality of an enterprise, it seems to the moralist, that requires commitment. It requires enlistment in what Josiah Royce called a cause. It requires an act of devotion, a kind of declaration of loyalty, beyond all interest, all personal motivation by curiosity, all love of gain or status or power and all kindred desires in men. The oath taken by the scientist has not been formalized as the physician's oath has been, or the statesman's or the clergyman's. But a similar commitment is involved. The scientist qua scientist enters into a covenant. He promises himself and promises the community of scientists that he will not allow his natural desires for all kinds of personal profits to interfere fundamentally with his service to his cause—the search for true knowledge. One does not hear much nowadays about scientific "disinterestedness." It was indeed a lame phrase for the idea. But it referred in a negative way to this fundamental moral element in the basis of science. It seems to the moralist that science requires of the scientist the sort of marriage ceremony in which the man says to science, his beloved, "I not only love you; I not only am attracted by you but I commit myself to you; leaving all other attractions I will cleave to you." This commitment has its emotional accompaniments of course. But it is not an emotion passively experienced. It is the sort of moral act to which a man can be true or false in a sense different from the way in which any scientific *theory* or *proposition* can be true or false.

This is the first point that strikes the moralist as he regards the scientist and his activities. Michael Polanyi in his effort to understand the personal element that enters into all scientific knowledge has struggled to understand the meaning of this scientific commitment. He writes, " 'I believe, that in spite of the hazards involved, I am called upon to search for the truth and state my findings.' This sentence, summarizing my programme, conveys an ultimate belief, which I find myself holding."[5] And so he struggles to unravel all the implications contained in this unscientific fact in the life of a scientist. To the moralist there is nothing strange or wonderful—though there is something not yet wholly intelligible—in the presence of this fact, namely, that science does not explain itself but rests on a commitment, on a loyalty which is personal; that no matter how impersonal all the objects and ends of science, the scientist himself remains even in science a person of whom the moral act of devotion to a cause is required.

A second element in the morality of science closely connected with the first comes to the attention of the ethical thinker. He notes that, whatever the end products of this activity are, it is marked in its whole course by continual *self-examination* and *self-criticism*. It seems subject always to a kind of triple discipline. There is the scientific conscience of the individual scientist; there is in the second place the continual, established habit of social criticism in the scientific community or communities; there seems to be in the third place the conviction that the theories and ideas are subject to control by something objective, however hard it is to define the objective. In any case here is an activity that is subject to the operations of an enlightened, never-ceasing self-criticism, of a conscience. Here is no mere power-struggle; here no simple appeal to the opinion of the majority or of the powerful. A principle is operating with which the moralist is familiar as present in all activity. It is unusually well-developed in its special scientific sphere. One considers, for instance, how scientific conscience operates in psychologists who make the conscience encountered in human beings before them their object. Do they examine the rightness or wrongness of their own theories, one asks oneself, merely because they are aware of possible social criticism? Does their own scientific conscience operate in accordance with their theories of how conscience in general operates? However that may be, the conscientiousness of science in continual self-criticism within the sphere of science itself seems to be a basic feature of the whole scientific adventure. We note how when Max Planck undertook to reflect on the course of science this point seemed to strike him with peculiar force. "Surely," he said, "about these ultimate questions much will still be thought

---

[5] *Op. cit.*, p. 299.

and much be written, for paper is patient. Therefore we will the more unanimously and unreservedly emphasize what must at all times without exception be acknowledged by us and taken to heart: *That is in the first place conscientiousness in self-criticism, combined with endurance in battling for that which has been found to be true;* and in the second place the honest respect for the person of the scientific opponent, a respect that is not to be shattered by misunderstandings—and for the rest the calm confidence in the power of that word which for more than 1900 years has taught us to separate the false prophets from the true: By their fruits you shall know them."[6]

The quotation calls our attention to a third and a fourth aspect of scientific morality: the loyalty of science, as science, to truth in personal relations, first within the community of science itself, secondly within the human community in general. Truth, it seems, from the perspective of science, is a right relation between propositions, ideas, and theories on the one hand, and objective reality or phenomena on the other, or it may be a right relation among propositions, ideas, and theories. In any case, so far as the scientist seeks truth he seeks true knowledge in some meaning of that term. But as was recognized long ago true knowledge and true communication are two different things. It is not to be taken for granted that because a man has true knowledge he will communicate truly. As Socrates in Plato's dialogue *The Lesser Hippias* recognized to his puzzlement, it is the man who knows most truly who can lie most effectively and deceive most persuasively. But now for no scientifically established reason that I am aware of, the scientific community has been marked by faithfulness in *truth-telling* as well as in *truth-knowing*, in true communication as well as in true inquiry. It has practiced a singular obedience to the Hebrew commandment, "Thou shalt not bear false witness against thy neighbor"—no less than singular devotion to that true knowledge which for Greek appreciation was the key to all other excellences of life. That the two things are not immediately related is apparent to us from many considerations, among them the conflicts which arise in the scientific conscience when it is required by a society to be secretive about knowledge and the greater conflict when it is demanded that knowledge be used for purposes of deception. There is inevitable

6 Planck, "Die Einheit des physikalischen Weltbilds" in *Wege zur physikalischen Erkenntniss*, 4th ed., Leipzig, 1944, p. 24.

conflict, writes President Conant, "between the presuppositions of the scientist and the government official. . . . Secrecy and science are fundamentally antithetic propositions." But when we read further we note that the conflict is not between science as knowledge and national government as government; it is rather between the whole open, truth-telling tradition of science and the tradition of national government. To the moralist it seems that President Conant is speaking here of the *moral* tradition of the community of persons carrying on science and not of science as knowledge; it is to that tradition also that he refers when he goes on to say, "One cannot help wondering how long a large fraction of our scientific manpower can be employed in this atypical (i.e. secret and closed) scientific work without threatening the traditions that have made science possible."[7] The point is not simply that the activities of science "are shot through with value-judgments"[8] but rather that they are carried on in a community of persons who value truth not only as a kind of relation among propositions or between propositions and facts but as also a relation between persons.

This same observation applies also when we consider the status of the scientific community in more inclusive human society. The moral tradition of science has enforced obedience to the common rule to speak truth to the scientific neighbor. But it has also been a tradition of honesty in relation to the larger community. How not to deceive his fellow men is often a problem for the scientist no doubt. But his very warnings to a layman that all the popularizations of his theories are myths and parables is an indication of his determination not to deceive. When the moralist thinks of the high status that science enjoys in the modern world he cannot help but ask whether one reason for it does not lie in the simple moral fact that scientists have commended themselves as trustworthy in their communication—in part by their very willingness, indeed their eagerness, to have their errors brought to light. Doubtless, confidence in modern as in ancient wise men is created in part by their ability to produce signs and miracles, and in part by the fact that events justify their predictions. But it is also created by their truthfulness which comes to light in the willingness to confess error. A scientific error and a personal lie are two kinds of evil widely removed from

[7] James B. Conant, *Modern Science and Modern Man*, 1952, pp. 13, 16, 30.
[8] *Ibid.*, p. 62.

each other. Scientists are aware of their constant effort to eradicate error; they do not always seem to be equally conscious of the discipline carried on in their community which fights against the lie, among themselves and in their more inclusive social relations.

The moralist who reflects on science in this way cannot divide human activities into a series of functions of which science is one, morality another. Morality is not something that can be institutionalized as science, art, education, medicine, and religion are institutionalized. It pervades all activities. Morality is present in the activity of science itself, as well as in the activity of artistic creation, or of religious proclamation, or of government. The question the moralist raises is not whether such science is in conflict with morality, but whether such science is adequately aware of its own moral character and whether scientists are sufficiently philosophic or comprehensive in their outlook so as to be able to order their activity as moral within the whole complex of human personal activities. The problem is important for him because of the vast respect science enjoys and because of the leadership it exercises in the modern world.

When I say that science is itself morally ordered by commitment to true and universal knowledge as a cause, by conscientiousness in self-criticism, and by faithfulness in truth-telling, I do not mean, of course, that it is not often in conflict with other codes and mores. There has been conflict between the morality of science and the morality that makes national survival an ultimate cause, or the morality that makes the maintenance of a system of religious dogma a final object of devotion. I have no doubt that there are more subtle conflicts between the morality of science and, for instance, the morality of medicine—the kind of conflict many a medical novel such as Sinclair Lewis' *Arrowsmith* dramatizes. There are the conflicts also within the scientist between his vocational devotion and his personal, individual interest. Surely the study and laboratory no less than a monastery can furnish the stage on which man's perennial moral battle for integrity is enacted. But all this is to speak of conflict among moralities and not of conflict between science and morality.

Neither can we speak of conflict between the moral tradition of science and the major moral tradition of Western society. Science within its own domain displays many of the features of that morality at its best. It is perhaps the most notable example of what has been regarded by some men as the characteristic of the Western —the Judaic-Christian—style of life, namely, the openness to new-ness, the nondefensiveness, the desire for *metanoia*, of change of mind. It embodies in its own way also the respect for being, the affirmation of what is, the positive valuation of existent reality, which Western religion seeks to express by speaking of creation. It is in principle universal as the Western moral tradition is in princi-ple universalistic. Its intent is always to find the truth that is uni-versally true and to state it in universal language. It carries on its activity in a universal society. In these respects and others science instead of being in conflict with morality is, as itself a moral enter-prise, an illustration of Western morality at its best, though in a particular sphere.

Yet the question arises whether the effect of this science has been indeed that of making us, in the society so largely influenced by it, more sensitive to our ultimate goods and obligations, and whether it has encouraged in nonscientific communities the adop-tion of moral disciplines correlate to those of science itself. To be sure, it is impossible to distinguish at all clearly the effects of science on the morality of modern man from the effects of many other in-fluences that abound in our highly complex situation. Science in social life is so closely associated with technology and the economic activities accompanying the latter that we cannot accurately de-termine its independent moral influence. We can consider only some few features of modern morality and ask what bearing science and scientific morality may have had on them.

The first of these features to which attention has been called many times is the tendency of modern men to live and act in a series of moral spheres that are not connected with each other. When in 1929 Walter Lippmann pointed to the situation in his *Preface to Morals* he described the movements of secession that had broken up the republic of human action into a series of in-dependent states. Wealth was pursued in one for wealth's sake, art in another for art's sake, truth in a third for truth's sake. Religion had also founded its own separate province. Since then the situation has not changed for the better, save insofar as the imposition of national morality, for which all other ends are subordinated to national survival and glory, may be regarded as an improvement. The prevalence of this national morality has offered to all the other provincial moralities their greatest challenge. It seeks, more or less consistently, to order all the obligations and value commitments of intellectual, artistic, religious, economic, and sometimes even domestic activity into the service of one cause. Insofar it is unifying. But insofar as science, art, religion, and economics have been implicitly universal in their orientation nationalism has been destructive. The moral division of our modern world has therefore a strangely double nature. On the one hand, we have divided our activities and the moral disciplines of those activities in a kind of horizontal fashion, as activities carried on in a universal community but without real correlation with each other. On the other hand we have tried to unite these activities but under the auspices of devotion to a nonuniversal, a national cause. Has science contributed anything to this situation? Perhaps this, that the success of its single-minded devotion to the separate end of true knowledge has encouraged among us the thought that such moral specialization is the way to the attainment of our human hopes. If so much true understanding can be gained by seeking knowledge only, is it not clear that all of us—in art, in economics, in religion—ought also to confine ourselves to one defined end? While science bears no direct responsibility for the compartmentalization of other modern moralities of action it has furnished an example to these other special communities. One of the challenges to scientists that they become philosophers arises out of this situation.

Another feature of modern man's morality also is not to be traced to science directly but to the use our society has made of it; this is the tendency among us to abandon large areas of our human existence to the sway of power, emotion, psychological drives, or pure force of one kind or another. This tendency is expressed in certain philosophical movements that purportedly build on science and undertake to use what they believe to be scientific methods in philosophy. In the most extreme statements of such philosophies only man's activity as knower of his world is regarded as really subject to the discipline of reason. Only scientific statements can be true or false. The political statements we make or our religious, moral, and aesthetic judgments are simply expressions of emotion. This philosophic movement, however, is only the intellectual accompaniment and perhaps justification of a general movement in modern morality that confines the work of reason—that is the work of seeking proportion, coherence, and law—to our activity as knowers while it regards our other activities—from sex to politics—as really outside our rational control. Judgments about true and false, about right and wrong, can be passed it is thought on the consequences of scientific action. But all other action is really beyond the sphere of such judgment and regarded as subject to chance or blind play or blind forces.

Can science be held responsible in any way for this tendency of modern man to surrender large areas of his existence and activity to irrationality? Perhaps it can partly and to the extent that its followers have not only sought true knowledge, but have also believed or proclaimed that true knowledge is complete truth, that no other truth, no other true relations, are necessary. To the extent that science has not honored or been conscious of the work of reason in other realms than those of knowledge, to the extent that it has claimed a certain monopoly on reason, it seems to bear some responsibility for the situation. One must add at once, of course, that on the whole it has not been the scientific community itself, but the nonscientific glorifiers of scientific reason who have most decried moral, artistic, and religious activity as beyond the scope of reason. The situation, however, does seem to call on scientists to become philosophers who will undertake to understand not only their own rational activity but the work of reason in all areas of human action, as observer's reason and as agent's reason, as objectively and subjectively directed reason, as reason seeking not only to know what is true and false but what is good and evil, just and unjust, wise and foolish.

When we think of the morality of modern man the point that strikes us most forcibly is the difficulty he has in thought and practice of doing justice to what he acknowledges to be the highest mundane values—the persons, the selves. Our Western morality is built on the recognition that nothing is more important, more to be served and honored, apart from God himself, than human I's and Thou's—the selves we are and the selves among whom we live. But the morality of personal worth maintains itself in our subconscious or conscious minds like an alien in a strange country where no one understands and few acknowledge his presence. These selves among selves are required to direct their attention to things, to impersonal powers, forces, relations, and concepts. They are the knowers, but only the known is acknowledged and honored; they devote themselves to the cause of knowledge, but only the publicly, generally present is accorded the recognition of being real and valuable. These selves are true and false to themselves and to one another, but only the truth and falsity of their statements about things assumed to be objective is considered important. They live in the intense subjectivity of decision, of anxiety about meaning, of commitment to their causes. They live in faithfulness and in treason. They must deal in their isolation with the questions of life and death, of being or not being. They must enact the dramas of devotion to great and little causes, suffer the spiritual pains of betrayal and being betrayed, of reconciliation to life and of revolt.

But as selves they are epiphenomena in the dominant world view of our society. Poetry and religion may portray them, but poetry and faith are officially regarded as dealing with the mythical. What alone is acknowledged, accepted as actual, is the object. So far as selves can be made objects—set before the mind as projected, external realities—they have their place. But then they are no longer selves; they are not I's and Thou's but It's.

So we live in a depersonalized and often disenchanted world in which we are taught to doubt the primary realities that we experience—the self and its companion selves, and in which we are taught to flee from the knowledge which lies near the beginning of wisdom —the knowledge of ourselves. Whenever we come near to accepting its challenge we are tempted to convert it into something else, namely, into the knowledge of something objective and generic— the knowledge of man in general or the knowledge of the operation of psychological forces.

The depersonalized world of modern man, the world in which all selves become objects for objective knowledge on the one hand, for objective manipulation in the market and the political arena on the other, is not a world in which the morality of personal value can flourish. It is not one in which the most difficult of all human inquiries is encouraged—the inquiry into good and evil and the examination of the self in its truth to itself and to others. It tends to become as "demoralized" as it is depersonalized.

Science certainly cannot be charged with responsibility for having brought forth this depersonalized, this devalued, this demoralized common world of ours. Yet insofar as the scientist has not been a philosopher who has been aware of the limits of his objectifying work, of the need of its complementation by the work of others devoted to truth of another sort than his truth, insofar as he has presented his objective world as the real world, insofar as he has been unaware of the moral element in his own activity, he bears some share in our common failure.

The human problem of our time cannot be stated by the use of such phrases as "science in conflict with morality." Our situation is not one of conflict between great forces. It is better described as a situation of emptiness. Life for man has become empty because it is without great purposes and great hopes and great commitments, without a sense of participation in a great conflict of good and evil. We shall not emerge out of this situation by passing judgments on one another in our various communities and callings, nor by trying to find out which one of us—scientific community, or economic, or religious or political—has led the rest of us astray. But we are challenged in all these spheres to become something more than we have been, not scientists only, nor logicians only, nor theologians only, but philosophers, lovers, and seekers of that inclusive wisdom which is an affair of whole selves in a whole world.

Index

Aristotle, 105, 111
Atheism, 24-25
Ayer, A. J., 101

Bentham, J., 101
Bergson, H., 25, 35
Buber, Martin, 41

Calvin, John, 116
Calvinism, 72
Catholicism, 72
Christianity: dilemma of radical monotheism in, 62; drive to universality in, 62-63; relational value theory in, 111-112
Clarke, Samuel, 34
Comte, Auguste, 35
Conant, James, 85, 135
Covenants: between man and God, 41-42; sacredness of, 72
Creed, support of, and science, 83

Democracy: development of, and the Transcendant, 95-96; question of, henotheistic or monotheistic, 77; radical monotheistic idea of, 96
Desire, and the good, 107-108
Durkheim, E., 88

Edwards, Jonathan, 116
Empiricism, value-centers in, 109-110
Epicureanism, 28-29
Equality: democratic dogma of, 73-77; challenge to doctrine of, 74-75; and faith expressions, 76-77
Ethics: in relation to scientific activity, 131; social faith and, 26-27
Existentialism, 29

Faith: as confidence and fidelity, 16-23; criticism of, 15; in God and in gods, 114-126; illumination of character of, 12-14; monotheistic and social, struggle between, 68-72; in the person, 44; Protestant, 116-119; radical, incarnation of, 39-42; reasoning in, 14-15; and revelation, 42-44; rival forms of, and democracy, 77; in science, 79-83.
Fascism, 27
Free Man's Worship, A, 123
Freedom, religious, 69-71

Gilson, Etienne, 42, 44
God: as object of faith, 12-13, 119; as source of being, 32-33, 38, 43, 122-123; as personal, 44 ff; and Jesus Christ, 42, 59, 124-125; and problem of existence, 114 ff.
Good: distinguished from right, 108-109; duality of, 105-106; as a function of desire, 107-108; problem of knowledge of, 107-108

Hartmann, Nikolai, 111
Henotheism, 11, 25-28; in American political and religious life, 71; in Christianity, church-centered or Christ-centered, 58-60; non-nationalist versions of, 27; prayer in, 54; sense of the holy in, 51-52; struggle in political life of monotheism with, 69
Holy, sense of the, 51-56
Humanism: bases of, 74; as a kind of henotheism, 35; modern, as a protest against henotheism, 88-89

"Incarnation," 40
Israel; see Judaism

Jesus Christ, 39-40, 42; as center of loyalty, 59-60; as revelation of God, 43-44; and transfer of faith to ultimate being, 124-125
Job, 47
Judaism: centered in the law, 60-61; dilemma of, 61; relational value theory in, 111-112; struggle between social henotheism and radical monotheism in, 57-58

Kant, Immanuel, 34, 116
Kierkegaard, 116, 123
Knowledge, as a value-center, 111

Lesser Hippias, The, 134
Lewis, Sinclair, 136
Life: as value-center, 36-37; in evolutionary ethics, 110-111
Lippmann, Walter, 31, 137
Loyalty, 18, 21-22; in national existence, 65-68; of scientists to the human community, 80-81
Luther, Martin, 116, 119-122

Marxism, as a religion, 27
Molière, Jean Baptiste, 19
Monotheism: in American political and religious life, 71; central and relative value systems in, 112-113; in the life of the Hebrews, 40-41; see also Radical monotheism
Moore, G. E., 100
Moral behavior, 26
Morality: its abandonment to irrationality, 138-139; and personal worth, 139-140
Moses, 39, 40
My Confession, 19

Nation states, religious and political loyalty in, 65-67
National Socialism, 27
Nationalism, 35; as a faith, 17-18, 27
Naturalism, 35-36

Personal Knowledge, 128
Planck, Max, 133-134
Plato, 100, 134
Pluralism, 28; of gods, self, and society, 30-31
Polanyi, Michael, 128, 131, 132-133

Politics, Western radical faith in, 64, 65
Polytheism, 29-30, 95, 118-121; prayer in, 54; sense of the holy in, 51
Pope, Alexander, 16
Prayer and reverence, conversion of, 50-56
Preface to Morals, 137

Radical monotheism, 31-37; compared with nonradical mixed forms of faith, 34-35; and confidence in the principle of being, 89; prayer in, 54; sense of the holy in, 52; and universal loyalty, 33-34; in Western religion, 38-39
Redemption, doctrine of, 55
Religion: efforts to define, 49-50; as a matter of covenant, 41-42; organized, radical faith in, 56-63; sociological analysis of, 25-26
Revelation, 43-44; and faith, 42-44; principle of personlike integrity in, 46-47
Reverence and prayer, conversion of, 50-56
Reverence for life, 36
Royce, Josiah, 18, 21-22, 132

St. Paul, 47, 55-56
Santayana, George, 89
Schleiermacher, Friedrich, 116
Schlick, Moritz, 101, 105
Schweitzer, Albert, 36
Science: closed-society orientation of, 84-86; commitment of, 131-132; in conflict with morality, 127-141; and depersonalized world of modern man, 140-141; faiths in, 79 ff; under henotheistic faith, 81-82; as illustration of Western morality, 136-137; and loyalty to truth in personal relations, 134-135; morality of, 130-131, 133; trust-loyalty syndrome in, 78; and unity of the world of being, 86-87
Shakespeare, William, 19
Sidgwick, Henry, 34
Social God, and many Gods, 24-31
Socrates, 134

Themis, 26
"Theocracy," 72